# TRAINING
## AND
# DEVELOPMENT
# COMPETENCE

## A
## PRACTICAL
## GUIDE

## Jill Brookes

**KOGAN
PAGE**

First published in 1995

Apart from any fair dealing for the purposes of research or private study, or criticism or review, as permitted under the Copyright, Designs and Patents Act, 1988, this publication may only be reproduced, stored or transmitted, in any form or by any means, with the prior permission in writing of the publishers, or in the case of reprographic reproduction in accordance with the terms of licences issued by the Copyright Licensing Agency. Enquiries concerning reproduction outside those terms should be sent to the publishers at the undermentioned address:

Kogan Page Limited
120 Pentonville Road
London N1 9JN

© Jill Brookes, 1995

**British Library Cataloguing in Publication Data**
A CIP record for this book is available from the British Library.

ISBN 0 7494 1462 6

Typeset by BookEns Ltd, Royston, Herts.
Printed and bound in Great Britain by Biddles Ltd, Guildford and King's Lynn.

# Contents

# Acknowledgements

To Reg Brookes for his skill in producing illustrations, for being my unofficial editor and proofreader and for his constant belief that I could actually write this book. To my students, past and present. To my colleagues Sue Browell and Ian Shell for their unstinting encouragement. Special thanks go to Dr Philip Dobson for his support in keeping me fit enough to write.

# Preface

The impetus to write this book was prompted by the rapid changes taking place in training and development as a result of the move towards competence-based training. The book has been written primarily for those trainers and developers who are working towards an NVQ or SVQ in training and development at Level 3 or Level 4. However, it may also be of particular value to four other major groups of people:

- those trainers who, while not working towards an NVQ or SVQ themselves, may be supporting learners who are following a competence- or outcome-based route in their own occupational area;
- training consultants, or those aspiring to that role;
- supervisors and line managers in the workplace who are becoming increasingly involved in the development and assessment of their staff as a result of competence- or outcome-based training;
- students of employee development or human resource development, for example, those working towards graduateship of the Institute of Personnel and Development or a Diploma in Human Resource Management.

The book aims to provide a framework of knowledge to support the development of those involved in the training and development function. It is practical in orientation with each chapter providing the opportunity for you to carry out activities in order to extend your knowledge. It does not concern itself with academic debate as it concentrates on putting theory into practice. What it does provide is extensive suggestions for further reading for those who wish to study a particular aspect in more depth. This allows you to 'pick and choose' according to your existing knowledge and skill.

The training culture that is increasingly embracing outcome-led development is still in its infancy compared to the traditional training and development culture and can require a major shift in skills, knowledge and attitude. This book aims to lead you through that process by supporting the development of your knowledge.

JILL BROOKES
September 1994

# 1

# Developing competence

## HOW TO USE THIS BOOK

There are a number of ways in which you can use this book, depending on your needs. You can use it to:

1. Develop your knowledge of current processes in training and development.
2. Provide evidence of knowledge for assessment to include in your portfolio for an NVQ or SVQ Level 3 or 4 in training and development.
3. Supplement your existing knowledge.
4. Provide you with a desk reference to current training and development practice.
5. Prepare you, as a line manager and potential assessor, for the changes taking place in training and development.

Each chapter includes an introduction, summary, references (where appropriate) and further useful reading list. Interspersed with the main text are activities designed to help you assess your knowledge of the particular topic under discussion when applied to your working environment. The activities are especially valuable if you are working towards an NVQ or SVQ in training and development as they can provide you with evidence of knowledge to supplement the evidence provided by your performance in the workplace. Evidence of knowledge is often difficult to obtain, especially that which demonstrates you have linked the theory to your current practice.

Most of the activities are followed by suggestions which support them, thus enabling you to obtain some feedback on your performance. The suggestions are not definitive answers, however, but merely provide you with some guidelines. Your answers will depend on many factors, for example:

- your role;
- your organization;
- the role of the training function;
- your understanding;
- current practice;
- types of training you are involved in.

Although the book aims to provide a framework of knowledge and understanding it is very much a practical text. It can therefore be of value to anyone concerned with the training and development function. This includes:

- the lone trainer;
- the consultant;
- the line manager;
- the assessor;
- the personnel officer;
- the training specialist;
- the training manager.

As each person using this book will already have different levels of skill and knowledge in the areas of training and development each chapter is supplemented with an extensive, and often detailed, list of further useful reading. This will enable you to decide, on the basis of your current knowledge of a particular topic, which areas you need, or would like, to study in more depth.

## THE CHANGING NATURE OF DEVELOPMENT

Traditionally, training and development has been focused on 'courses', however, with the growth of outcome- or competence-based development, many changes are taking place. The focus is shifting to competence and 'competences', referred to in the USA as 'competencies'. The concern in the UK has therefore shifted from the process of training and development to the assessment of the outcomes of such development. This is just one of a number of differences between traditional and competence-based qualifications or awards. The major features are listed below.

| *Traditional* | *Competence-based* |
| --- | --- |
| Time-bound | Open-ended |
| Norm-referenced | Criterion-referenced |
| Percentage-rated | Not percentage-rated |
| Input-based | Outcome-based |

### Time-bound versus open-ended

Traditional courses and training interventions usually last a specified length of time, for example, in your experience the following may apply:

- assertiveness – 3 days plus a follow up day
- MBA – 1 year full time, 3 years part time

- presentation skills – 3 days
- robotics – 6 weeks.

The assumption behind these time-bound courses is that everyone learns at the same rate, and if they do not, then they will just have to work harder to catch up, or fail. Some examination-based qualifications allow a 'second sitting' if you fail a set assignment or examination, but for others no second chance is given.

Outcome- or competence-based qualifications or awards are open-ended, in that each individual learner proceeds at their own pace. This focus on the individual can result in very different patterns of progress through the qualification or award. It also recognizes existing skill and knowledge so that those who are more experienced in particular aspects of the award can progress more quickly through those areas. This can result in learners being more motivated as they are not having to sit through a training session on something they can already demonstrate competence in.

## Norm- versus criterion-referenced

Many traditional qualifications, awards or training interventions are graded on the basis of how well you have done compared to others in your group, set or class. This is norm referencing. The standard is set by the range of performance of the group. How well your individual performance is rated depends on the performance of everyone else, as there are no objective standards of measurement.

Outcome- or competence-based assessment depends on how well you have performed against a clearly specified set of objective standards. This is criterion referencing. It means that there are specific criteria against which the individual learner is measured. It does not depend on the performance of other people. As you can see, there are great benefits for both the learner and the trainer as the standards allow for objective assessment. Criteria for the assessment of competent performance are clearly laid down and can be applied to each individual. It is their performance judged against the standards and not their performance judged against the performance of others that is being assessed.

## Percentage-rated or not

Percentage-rated or pass/fail assessments are common in traditional courses or training interventions, and some are not formally assessed at all. This factor, added to the time-bound nature of the majority of programmes plus norm-referencing, can result in a higher failure rate than is justified.

However, outcome- or competence-based assessment relies on only three categories:

- competent;

- not yet competent;
- insufficient evidence to make a decision.

These categories are discussed in detail in chapter 10 (p. 211). When you add this factor to the open-ended nature of the award, then there are obvious benefits to the learner.

## Input- versus outcome-based

The emphasis on traditional programmes has usually been on inputs. By that I mean what the trainer and learners do and the syllabus or scheme of work, and this has largely been under the control of the trainer. The programme for the training intervention has been set and all the learners following a particular award or qualification have followed it. The outcomes have generally been variable as a result of the factors outlined above.

The focus on outcomes, however, clearly identified at the beginning of a programme or award, means that the emphasis is on individual learners and their progress. As a result of this not all learners will require the same inputs and individual learning plans are drawn up for each learner. These learning plans identify areas for development and the processes that are required to support that development. This requires different kinds of support from the trainer and others involved in the development process. These tasks are discussed in detail in chapter 3 (p. 46).

With these shifts in emphasis the whole nature of training and development is changing. That is not to say that the principles on which traditional training and development is based have changed, ie: identify the need; design the intervention; deliver the intervention; then evaluate the outcomes. What it does mean is that there are some additional tasks or processes required as a result of this shift. As a consequence trainers, consultants, line managers, training managers and others involved in the human resource development process are themselves having to develop new competences in order to support learners who are undertaking competence-based qualifications or awards.

## THE FORMAT OF STANDARDS

In the UK there is a new system of qualifications leading to a National Vocational Qualification (NVQ). In Scotland they are known as Scottish Vocational Qualifications (SVQs). They follow the same format and are constructed from competence-based standards. An NVQ is:

*A statement of competence relevant to employment. It is this statement which specifies the competence to be achieved ... It is the basis from which assessment procedures, recording and certification are derived.*

*(NCVQ 1988)*

NVQs are comprised of a number of units of competence and each unit contains the following:

- elements;
- performance criteria;
- range statements;
- knowledge requirements;
- performance evidence.

This is graphically illustrated in Figure 1.1.

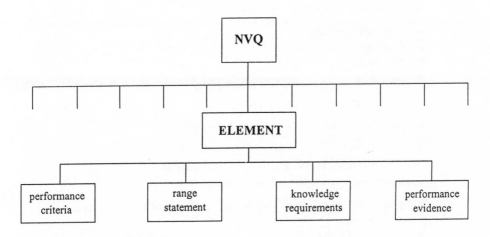

**Figure 1.1** *NVQ structure*

These components will now be addressed in more detail using the information in Figure 1.2 as an example. Figure 1.2 is an excerpt from the first-line (Management 1) occupational standards for managers produced by the Management Charter Initiative.

**Unit 1 9 Exchange information to solve problems and make decisions**

**Element 1 9.3 Advise and inform others**

*Performance Criteria:*
(a) Advice and information to aid and assist others is offered and disseminated at an appropriate time and place
(b) Information given is current, relevant and accurate
(c) Information is presented in a manner, and at a level and pace appropriate to the receiver
(d) Advice is consistent with organisational policy and cost and resource constraints
(e) Advice is supported, as appropriate, by reasoned argument and evidence.

*Range Indicators:*
Advice and information is offered:

- proactively with the manager taking the initiative
- on request

Advice is based upon:

- knowledge
- expertise
- experience
- position in the organisation

Advice and information is given to:

- immediate manager
- colleagues, specialists, staff in other departments
- customers
- suppliers

Advice and information is given:

- verbally (either one to one or in groups)
- in writing

## PERFORMANCE EVIDENCE REQUIRED
Evidence must cover the following items from the range:

- advice and information offered proactively with the manager taking the initiative
- advice and information given verbally and in writing
- evidence of advice given to:
  the immediate manager
  colleagues, specialists and staff in other departments
  customers
  suppliers

## OTHER EVIDENCE
Reports, manuals, newssheets, articles, videos and audio/visual materials; supported by extensive witness testimony from line managers, colleagues, subordinates, customers and suppliers. This may be drawn from experiences and practices in a role as advisor to decision makers.

In the absence of sufficient evidence from performance alone, personal test/simulations or questioning to be used to gain additional evidence of presentational skills and understanding of the principles, methods relating to:

- seeking and exchanging information, advice and support
- organising and presenting information
- presenting a logical and clear argument which addresses the needs and priorities of recipients in a variety of situations

Crown Copyright (1991)

**Figure 1.2** *An example of UK occupational standards*

## Element

This is the smallest part of competence that can be assessed as part of an NVQ and it is a sub-division of a unit of competence. The element is always stated in precise terms and requires performance criteria to indicate exactly what is expected in terms of outcomes. It is a description of something that someone actually does in that occupational area (see the beginning of Figure 1.2).

## Performance criteria

Without performance criteria the requirements of the element could be interpreted in many ways. Performance criteria indicate the standard of performance required for the successful achievement of the element of competence. They are statements by which an assessor can judge whether or not the evidence of performance generated by the individual demonstrates competence in the activity specified by the element. They are therefore explicit statements of the outcomes required.

As you can see in Figure 1.2, they clearly specify what outcomes are required, and, those outcomes are clearly measurable and therefore assessable.

## Range statement

These are also sometimes called Range Indicators, as in the example in Figure 1.2. They describe the limits (or range of conditions) within which performance must be demonstrated for the individual to be assessed as competent. They act as a guide to the learner, the trainer or developer and the assessor and are designed to reflect the breadth and depth of a particular occupational role.

They therefore give explicit detail about the range of conditions attached to the demonstration of the performance criteria, and, thus, the element, and ultimately, the unit.

## Knowledge requirements

As different occupational standards often have differing layouts this may not be an explicit heading. For example, in Figure 1.2 the knowledge requirements are identified under 'Other Evidence', paragraph 2.

There is an assumption within the NVQ system that knowledge can be inferred from performance and the knowledge requirements are there to 'fill the gaps' that cannot be easily inferred. They could be viewed therefore as supplementary to the range statements.

## Performance evidence

This clearly states the evidence that the assessor requires in order to make a decision about your competence. See the example from Figure 1.2. In this example there is also 'other evidence' of items that are products of performance. This is known as secondary evidence.

Performance evidence may also specify the number of times performance must be successfully assessed for the learner to be deemed competent.

If you wish to know more about the UK competence-based system and NVQs, see 'Further useful reading' at the end of this chapter.

## OVERVIEW

### Chapter 2

This gives you an overview of training in the context of the organization. It begins by looking at the theories of culture and structure and relates them to the organization you are working within. At this stage it also helps you to identify where the training function 'fits' within your organization. It then moves on to identify the systematic training cycle and how you can use it to promote the training function within the organization. Reasons for organizations investing in training are then considered and the possible symptoms and causes of performance problems are discussed and linked to the training cycle.

### Chapter 3

This concentrates on the different roles of those involved in the training and development function. It does this by identifying the four major spheres of training activity and relating them to your everyday performance. A major focus of chapter 3 is on the additional tasks that trainers are required to perform as the result of the introduction of outcome- or competence-based training and development. It explores the implications of this for current practice and the resultant focus on the individual learner. The final part of this chapter concentrates on the giving and receiving of feedback, as the importance of this skill is highlighted throughout the book.

### Chapter 4

The focus here is on learning. It explores the role that learning plays within a training intervention and identifies the four major ways that people learn. You are encouraged to explore your own training practice to identify which methods you use for a particular intervention. This leads on to the experiential learning cycle and how it is essential for effective learning to take place. As a consequence of this learning styles are discussed, along with their implications for training interventions. This knowledge is then used to help you design a strategy for a design brief for a training intervention.

Occupational standards are then discussed along with other kinds of outcome-based qualifications or awards. In particular, their impact on training and development and their relationship with performance is highlighted. As a result of this the process of developing learning outcomes is discussed in the context of occupational or organizational standards and performance problems.

## Chapter 5

The factors influencing the choice of training intervention is the first port of call for chapter 5. It then moves on to examine, in some detail, the different types of intervention strategy. They are broadly categorized into 'on-the-job' and 'off-the-job' methods. Another factor affecting the choice of intervention is the learner. The entry behaviour of learners is discussed in detail along with some strategies for ascertaining it prior to the intervention. Another important aspect is the development of resources to support the learner and this is explored in depth, from the development of visual aids through to support mechanisms for learners. Finally, the crucial issue of learning transfer is identified along with its implications for the development and delivery of the training intervention.

## Chapter 6

This chapter begins by looking at the reasons why trainers should get involved in the process of organizational training-needs analysis. The benefits of training-needs analysis for the trainer and the organization are identified. This includes the need for any training intervention to be relevant and this aspect is explored along with other reasons for the organization to carry out a training-needs analysis. Organizational training-needs analysis is then discussed in depth and a checklist supplied. Turning the knowledge gained from the analysis into a table of priorities and then into an organizational training plan rounds off this section. The final section in chapter 6 explores individual training needs analysis and methods for carrying this out. Chapter 6 therefore explores training needs at both a macro (organizational) and micro (individual) level.

## Chapter 7

Strategic and operational planning is the focus of this chapter: both the theoretical and practical aspects are discussed here. It also offers you the opportunity to demonstrate your competence by putting an operational plan into practice. Budgeting is explored next and its importance to the organization, coupled with strategic and operational planning, is identified. The next step in the process is the identification of appropriate training and development options and their associated resources to support identified aspects of the plan. The allocation of identified resources and the issues that this raises for you as a trainer and developer, consultant or training manager are then discussed. The final section considers the effects of change and its potential effects on your implementation plan.

## Chapter 8

Chapter 8 can help you develop your role from one of simply developing and delivering. Consulting and advising covers a range of generic skills that anyone involved in training and development will find essential. The chapter begins by identifying the opportunities you have for working informally within an organization. As a result of this a number of key skill areas are identified, they include:

- effective presentations;
- contributing to meetings;
- presenting written information;
- record keeping;
- interviewing;
- effective negotiation;
- information gathering.

Chapter 8 concludes by identifying the opportunities you have for consulting and advising within the organization.

## Chapter 9

Quality is a key issue in training and development and chapter 9 explores how quality can be identified and maintained through the use of evaluation. It begins by looking at the reasons why organizations, training departments, and trainers and developers should evaluate the outcomes of both training interventions and individual development. It goes on to explore some methods of evaluation and the various stages at which these can take place. Identifying the costs and benefits of training and development, and the difficulties associated with this, are then discussed. Following on from this is a section identifying how you can use the results of evaluation to promote the training and development function, and tangibly demonstrate your effectiveness. The final section explores how you can incorporate innovations and developments into existing practice in order to maintain both the quality and currency of your interventions.

## Chapter 10

This final chapter concentrates on the processes and issues surrounding the assessment of outcome- or competence-based training and development. It begins by looking at the key roles involved in assessment and verification before moving on to outline the assessment process. One of the key differences between traditional and outcome-based training and development is identified next: assessment in the workplace. The role the assessor plays in the collection and assessment of evidence follows and second line assessment is then discussed. The final section addresses the effective recording of assessment decisions.

## References

MCI (1991) *Occupational Standards for Managers*, MCI, London.
NCVQ (1988) *Information Note 4 (November)*, NCVQ, London.

## Further useful reading

The following are all general reference books and may also be listed in other chapters:

Buckley, R and Caple, J (1994) *The Theory and Practice of Training*, third edition, Kogan Page, London.

Fletcher, S (1994) *NVQs, Standards and Competence*, second edition, Kogan Page, London.

Harrison, R (1992) *Employee Development*, IPM, London.

Prior, J (ed.) (1991) *Gower Handbook of Training and Development*, Gower, Aldershot.

Reid, M, Barrington, H and Kenney, J (1992) *Training Interventions*, third edition, IPM, London.

Truelove, S (ed.) (1992) *Handbook of Training and Development*, Blackwell, Oxford.

# 2

## Training and the organization

### INTRODUCTION

Training does not occur in a vacuum. It's not something we can just take down from a shelf, use and put back again. Because of this there are all kinds of things influencing what we do as trainers, when we do them and how we do them. This is because we all work within, or for, organizations, and organizations have different structures and different cultures.

This chapter identifies the interaction between the organization and its people and what the implications of this may be for the training function. We begin this process by examining the cultures and structures of organizations.

You may already be familiar with the terms but if you are not, then the definitions below will help.

> **Culture** usually refers to the set of norms, values, ideas and beliefs held about the way things are done (or not done!) in the organization. These things are often not written down.
> **Structure** refers to the way the organization is organized. This includes levels of responsibilities, task allocation, decision-making, etc. It could be referred to as the map of the organization.

As if this were not enough, we also have to take into consideration that organizations are not just a collection of norms, values, departments or functions. They are actually made up of individuals. These may share the norms and values and belong to departments or functions but they are all unique. So not only do we have demands made upon us by the culture and structure of the organization, we also have to deal with *people*. We cannot afford, therefore, to look at training as simply something that we perform from day to day. To become more competent and therefore more effective as trainers we need to begin to look at wider issues and start asking some questions (see the Activity box).

## ACTIVITY

Below are some examples of the kinds of questions we need to ask to begin to understand the context within which we train. Please try to answer as many of the questions as you can now, and add others that you would like to ask.

- Why does my organization invest in training?
- How important is the role of training in my organization?
- Who decides what training is to happen, when and for whom?
- Who benefits from my company's training?
- What would happen to my organization if it didn't train?
- How do the people we train feel about the training provided by our organization? Is it a punishment or a reward, a necessary evil or a right?
- What kinds of things outside the organization affect the training we do?
- How is the training in my organization planned. Is it systematic, does it help meet my organization's business objectives, has it got an adequate budget, or does it seem to 'just happen'?
- What role do I play in my organization's training?
- What skills do I need?

Some questions in the box may have been easier to answer than others. There may even be some questions that you can't answer yet. As you work through the rest of this chapter however, you should gain a broader understanding of the role training plays in your organization as well as the people and events that influence it. It also helps to involve other people in your organization who can provide you with this and other training-related information. This way you can begin to build up a useful network of contacts. The importance of building up such a network is explored in more detail in chapter 3 (p. 45)

It is very tempting to look at training as something that you just *do*! It is much more difficult, and challenging, to look at *why* you do it. Looking at yourself as a member of the organization as well as a trainer will make it easier for you to do this.

## THE ORGANIZATION

This section, will help you begin to see yourself as a member of the organization as well as a trainer or consultant by introducing you to different kinds of organization cultures and structures. This will enable you to identify the prevalent or main culture present within your organization. You will also be able to draw a map of your own organization based on your current experience and the models presented here.

How many times, in the course of your work, do you stop and think about the organization you are working in? Do you just take it for granted as something that is 'there'? Have you ever tried to find the rule book that says 'in this organization we do it this way'? The book that tells you how to relate to the people around you, how to deal with mistakes, whom you can talk to, whether you can have a cup of coffee at your desk. The list is endless. It is almost like a book of etiquette, except it is not written down!

This is also one of the most difficult challenges a newcomer to an organization faces, whether they are a new member of staff or a trainee from another department. And it is also difficult because, after a while, there are things you 'take for granted' because 'everyone knows that you don't stand talking in the corridors, or that you don't just have a cup of coffee when you feel like it'. But where does it say this?

This, in simple terms, is what is referred to as your organization's culture. In some books you will also see it referred to as the organizational climate. It is all the things you come to learn after spending time in an organization. On entering an organization for the first time you may be given an introductory handbook and there will also be terms and conditions formalized in your contract of employment. These are the *official* rules of the organization, but, as you spend more time there you realize that the organization has certain characteristics and you become socialized into them. By that I mean that you learn them as you go along until they become 'unconscious', and that is why they can be difficult to identify (see the Activity box).

## ACTIVITY

Try to identify the 'unwritten rules' in your organization. It may help if you 'visualize' your organization by giving it a person's name or by likening it to a particular animal. Once you have done this you need to identify why you feel this way about it.

You have probably identified quite a wide range of 'unwritten rules', some of which encourage you to do more than is contractually required of you and some that encourage you to do less. Some examples include:

- Routinely working after 5 pm.
- Being at your desk early every morning.
- Not taking your full lunch break.
- Not taking coffee breaks.
- Taking work home.
- Not being 'off sick'.
- Going home early because it's Friday.

- Going to the dentist/doctor during work hours.
- Drinking coffee at your desk.
- Lunch takes as long as it takes.
- Being able to stop and speak to the MD.
- Wandering over to other departments to 'see what is going on'.
- Always being available to your manager.

As you can see from this list, some 'unwritten rules' work in your favour, others are more prohibitive. Again, the kind of unwritten rules there are in your organization depends on the culture, so let us look at some of the different kinds of cultures that can exist in organizations.

# CULTURES

Probably the best known work on organizational cultures is that of Charles Handy. He identified four major cultures:

- The *Power* Culture;
- The *Role* Culture;
- The *Task* Culture;
- The *Person* Culture.

Below you will find a brief explanation of each of these cultures which is derived from Handy's work.

## Power culture

This type of culture is usually found in small entrepreneurial organizations. It depends on a central power source, on trust and empathy for its effectiveness, and on mind-reading and personal conversation for its communication. There are few rules and procedures and little bureaucracy, as control is usually exercised by only one or two people. Decisions are usually taken by only a few people and are usually the outcome of the balance of power. This means that decisions are usually taken for political reasons rather than from logical analysis of the situation.

One of the benefits of this culture is that the organization has the ability to move quickly and can therefore react well to threat, danger or opportunity. It also places a lot of faith in the individual and little in committees. Individuals are judged by results and this creates a very competitive atmosphere. The organization is therefore ideally placed to manage change.

While it produces an organization that can react quickly to events, whether it reacts effectively will depend on the person or persons at the centre. The type of people who have best chance of survival in such a culture are those who are power-oriented, politically minded, and risk-taking and who rate job security low on their list of priorities.

## Role culture or bureaucracy

This type of culture is often referred to as a bureaucracy. However, because for many in our society a bureaucracy is seen as something negative, 'role' is used here. As it suggests, this type of culture is usually found in large organizations with many layers or levels to them. The organization is usually characterized by having specific departments or specialities, eg, finance, purchasing, production, training, maintenance or servicing.

Work is controlled by sets of procedures and rules. There are procedures for specific roles, with job descriptions and a 'pecking order', procedures for communications, rules for discipline and grievance, promotion and staff development, etc. These specialities are co-ordinated at the top by a narrow band of senior management or an executive board and decision-making relies heavily on the rules and procedures.

The benefits of such a culture are best seen where economies of scale are required and the organization operates in a market where technical expertise and depth of knowledge or specialization are more important than creativity or cost. This type of culture does not respond well to change, however. It can be slow to perceive the need for change and even slower to react when the need is seen. It can offer the individual security and predictability with little personal risk, as there is little room for individual responsibility or autonomy.

## Task or matrix culture

The task culture is job- or project-oriented and may be found where the market is extremely competitive, where products have a short life-span, or where you may carry out more than one role in the organization. Control is difficult in this kind of culture and usually depends on top management allocating the projects, people and resources. Little day-to-day control can be exerted once they have been allocated, however, as this would be seen as 'breaking the rules'.

One of the major benefits of this culture is its adaptability. It does have some major disadvantages too. It cannot produce economies of scale or great depth of expertise and it is also quite unstable, particularly when there is a shortage of resources. Decision-making can also be difficult. Despite this the task culture is the preferred choice to work in of most middle and junior managers as it focuses on group and team working and leadership skills.

## Person culture

This type of culture is quite unusual as it is found in organizations that are simply a group of people banding together to share resources while they all 'do their own thing'. Examples include accountancy partnerships, lawyers, dentists, general practitioners, independent training consultants and, sometimes, specialists within organizations. These last-named usually see the organization as something simply serving their own ends. Senior medical staff in hospitals are a good example of this.

The only rules and procedures are by mutual agreement and tend to be minimal. Decision-making is shared among the cluster of people making up this organization.

## Your organization's culture

What you need to be aware of, however, when attempting to apply the models to your organization is that the four cultures outlined above are very much 'Ideal Types'. This means that they are unlikely to be seen exactly as they are described here. Most organizations, especially larger ones, will show evidence of all four cultures. What is important is that you can identify the main or prevalent culture in your organization or even in different departments within the organization from the four presented above.

The key things you need to consider are:

- Who holds the power?
- What kinds of rules and procedures are there?
- What kind of decision-making is there?
- What are the benefits and weaknesses of the culture for your organization?
- What kind of people does it best suit?

---

### ACTIVITY

Write a short report identifying the prevalent culture in your organization. It will help if you refer to the key questions listed.

---

## TYPES OF STRUCTURE

Culture is not the only impact the organization has upon us. How the organization is structured can also have a major impact upon its people. It is also helpful to recognize how culture and structure relate to each other and one of the easiest ways to do this is to look at the structures typical of the four culture types outlined above.

## Power culture = web structure

This type of structure has a central power source, with rays of power and influence spreading out from the centre. Just like a spider's web (see Figure 2.1)

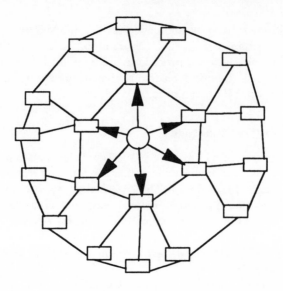

**Figure 2.1** *Web structure*

## Role Culture = hierarchical structure

This type of culture could also be likened to a pyramid (see Figure 2.2). A broad base of 'workers', co-ordinated by a lesser number of managers, who are co-ordinated by fewer managers, who are co-ordinated by even fewer senior managers, who are controlled by an executive board. The pyramid gets narrower as you move up the organization's hierarchy.

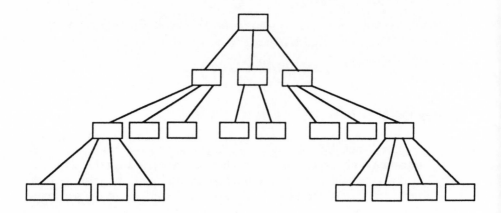

**Figure 2.2** *Pyramid structure*

## Task culture = matrix structure

In this kind of organization teams are brought together to carry out specific tasks while still having a line manager to whom they report (see Figure 2.3). A good example of this is a college. A college is split into a number of teaching areas, for example, accountancy, business studies, and marketing, and each of these areas has a head of department. But because the college is set up to teach a number of courses there is also a course leader in charge of each one.

If you are a lecturer you therefore report to:

(a) your head of department
(b) any course leaders whose courses you teach on.

It can get quite complicated sometimes though!

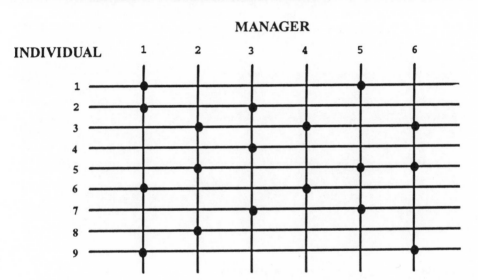

**Figure 2.3** *Matrix structure*

## Person culture = cluster structure

As you discovered earlier, this culture is an unusual one (see Figure 2.4). There is little formal structure as it is the minimum possible to support the work of the 'star' or 'stars'. If you have a number of these stars clustering together it could also be referred to as a galaxy of individual stars. Even so, alongside it the supporting structure may have its own culture.

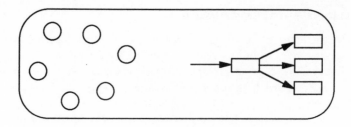

**Figure 2.4** *Cluster structure*

Now see the Activity box. It is likely that the diagram you produce will bear only an approximation to one of the structure types outlined above. That is all right. What is important, however, is that you are able to indicate where you fit into that structure, because where you are placed in the organization will affect the contribution you can make to its decision-making process for human resource development.

## ACTIVITY

Using the information you have now on the culture of your organization, or the organization you are acting as a consultant for, along with the descriptions above of the kinds of structures of organizations, first of all draw the organization's structure, then write a brief statement on where you fit into that structure.

## HOW IS TRAINING ORGANIZED?

For training and development to be successful it needs to be organized effectively. The organization needs to have and support a training department, or, at the very least, someone with dedicated responsibility for training within personnel. It is essential to have a training policy and training plan and to allocate a realistic budget to the training function, and for training and development to be represented and supported at board level. It is also important to recognize that training is not the solution to all problems, and, indeed, that it could sometimes simply exacerbate the situation, but we shall look at that in more detail in chapter 6 (p. 110)

Training is usually identified or associated with performance problems, either existing or potential, and therefore there needs to be a systematic framework to identify and support training interventions. (Training intervention is a term used to describe any training and development activity.)

## ACTIVITY

List the steps or stages that you think are required for effective and systematic training.

In doing the Activity exercise (see the box), you could have listed some of the following:

1.  Establish terms of reference.
2.  Job analysis.
3.  Knowledge and skills analysis.
4.  Analysis of target group.
5.  Training needs and content analysis.
6.  Develop criteria for assessment.
7.  Prepare training objectives.
8.  Consider and select training methods.
9.  Design and pilot training.
10. Deliver the training.
11. Internal validation.
12. External validation and evaluation.

These points can also be more simply represented by the 'training cycle' (see Figure 2.5).

## THE TRAINING CYCLE

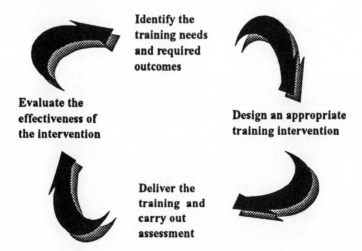

**Figure 2.5** *The training cycle*

In the UK the Training and Development Lead Body (TDLB) describes the key purpose of training and development as: 'To develop human potential to assist organizations and individuals to achieve their objectives.'

They have used the systematic training cycle to define areas of competence in training and development. They chose the training cycle because:

- it describes systematically and comprehensively the complete training and development process;
- it is familiar in all sectors and to all parts of the training community;
- most training and development roles can be located within it.

The training cycle has many applications and is based around the premise that we are helping people with current or potential performance problems. Subsequent chapters in this book look at each of these stages in more detail but each one is considered briefly here.

## Identifying training needs

Earlier performance problems, current or anticipated, have been briefly mentioned as the basis for many training interventions. The problems may be associated with an individual's current role or development towards a future one. Some may require major intervention, while others may be relatively minor.

The identification of training needs can help to improve performance as training is then a response to an identified and defined performance problem. If there isn't a performance problem then there is little or no justification for training.

Identification of training needs should therefore underpin *all* training and development interventions. There are a number of techniques that you can use to identify training needs and they are covered in detail in chapter 6 (p. 101). But it is also important to remember that training alone will rarely wholly solve a performance problem. For training interventions to be successful it is also necessary to identify the non-training needs relevant to the performance problem and include them in any proposed intervention. These non-training needs are usually technology- or systems-related.

### ACTIVITY

Briefly describe how training needs are identified in your organization.

## Plan and design training

This step in the systematic training cycle is concerned with the most effective use of resources available to address the identified training need. Some performance problems can be addressed using existing training provision; others require a new, innovative or creative approach involving specific planning, design and development.

The other major consideration at this stage is that any training interventions have to be planned within other constraints. These may be financial, resource, operational, staff availability, etc, but whatever they are, they have implications for the nature and scale of the intervention.

Planning a training intervention, whether it is for an individual or for a group of people, needs to focus on the outcomes required. The outcome is usually an improvement in performance; therefore, the training intervention is not complete until that improvement in performance is achieved. Increasingly, training is being seen in outcome terms and the focus is gradually shifting from the training process itself. This is where we, as trainers, need to be wary not to throw the baby out with the bath water. We still need to concern ourselves with the most effective process to achieve those outcomes, otherwise we risk a fall in the quality of our output.

With the increasing emphasis on measurable competence or performance capability we also need to recognize that courses are not the only form of training intervention at our disposal. Courses may be part of a wider training intervention, but on their own they are unlikely to meet all the performance problem requirements.

The major features, positive and negative, of courses are that:

- they are usually of fixed length regardless of individuals' needs;
- they are usually designed for a number of people with similarly perceived needs;
- they are usually general in focus and therefore not necessarily job or performance specific;
- in the short term they are usually cost effective.

The design aspect of training is simply the application of training technology to devising learning opportunities. If accurate and realistic objectives are set for the intervention then the design of the learning opportunity should closely match the achievement of those objectives. Now see the Activity box.

## ACTIVITY

What kinds of training interventions does your organization or department provide? What form do they take?

The kinds of intervention you describe in the Activity exercise will obviously be quite specific in terms of their objectives. The form they take, however, will probably include some of the following:

- action learning
- case studies
- skills development
- team building
- experiential learning
- group meetings
- coaching
- mentoring
- job changes

- learning contracts
- action planning
- computer-based training
- self development
- job instruction
- distance/flexible learning
- training courses
- development days

## Implement training

The successful implementation of training depends on many factors. They include the accurate identification of the training need and the participants' recognition of the need for training. Also essential is management support to help ensure that the intervention is at an appropriate level for the participants and the performance problem. You can also maintain or increase participation through the appropriate selection of learning methods and by ensuring that the trainer/developer possesses the right mix of training and technical skills to support individual learning needs.

It is often of vital importance that other members of staff are involved in the implementation process. In many cases the trainer will also be the line manager or technical specialist and without their involvement it is unlikely that satisfactory performance will be achieved quickly or effectively (see the Activity box).

Also of primary importance is the three-way interaction between the objective, the method, and the learner, that is, what has to be learnt, the means used to learn it, and the participant/recipient. All too often mismatches occur where one of these factors takes precedence over the others to the extent that the training becomes ineffective.

---

### ACTIVITY

Who is involved in implementing training in your organization?

---

Depending on your organization there may be a number of people involved. They could include trainers, consultants, the training manager, company directors, the learners themselves, customers, the personnel manager or personnel assistants and line managers.

## Evaluation

This next stage in the training cycle is perhaps the most important one, and also the one most usually neglected. It aims to answer the question: 'How beneficial has this intervention been?' As the purpose of a training or development intervention is usually to benefit the organization that is financing it, as well as the individuals participating, we need to be able to assess and evaluate the results obtained. In order to be able to do this we need to have made sure that we have designed the intervention in such a way as to produce measurable improvement. If we have clearly identified terms of reference with unambiguous objectives we should be able to identify successful outcomes.

So what is success? It usually means that:

- the learner or participant can do what is expected of them as a result of the intervention;
- their training or development needs have been met and any real or potential performance problem solved;
- the organization's investment in training is seen to be beneficial and effective;
- the trainers and the training department maintain credibility within the wider organization and may increase their power base.

---

### ACTIVITY

How does your organization determine whether or not training has been successful?

---

There are a number of ways in which your organization may already measure the effectiveness of its training interventions (see the Activity box). These may include the following:

- Learners/participants are asked to comment on the training they have received.
- Managers are asked to assess any subsequent improvement in performance following the intervention.
- The trainer/s assess the quality of the intervention and their performance.
- Customers are asked for feedback on the effectiveness of the intervention against the agreed terms of reference and objectives.

There are a wide range of internal and external validation and evaluation measures available and they are covered in chapter 9 (p. 177).

It seems appropriate to look now at why organizations invest in training, and, who potentially benefits from it.

## INVESTING IN TRAINING

Why do organizations bother with training? Can't we just rely on people learning for themselves? Why should we go to the trouble and expense of tying up human resources to plan, manage, organize, deliver and evaluate training, not to mention losing people's production while they learn 'off-the-job'?

There are a number of reasons to justify why we should not rely simply on an individual's ability to learn naturally.

- They are more likely to learn 'bad habits' or a way that is wrong.
- They may never be able to carry out the task competently.
- They may pose a health and safety risk, to themselves and to others.
- Once a task has been learned and practised incorrectly, it is difficult to unlearn and then relearn.
- Incompetent performance will usually result in poor quality outcomes.

All of the above can result in high hidden costs to the organization.

Hidden costs include customer complaints and rectification, high labour turnover, poor customer care, high reject rates, equipment down-time through misuse or poor maintenance, etc. These may be everyday occurrences in the organization, and, indeed, can sometimes be seen as part of the culture of the organization. This is potentially damaging to the organization in the medium to long term as these problems are often not seen as resulting from a lack of training.

Training is therefore very important in this context. If an organization relies wholly on the naturally occurring learning process, apart from the problems identified above, the organization may never be successful. Learning is also a critical success factor for an organization because if the sales force are not trained in a new product or service, or production staff in a new piece of equipment, or managers in their new technology, etc, then the learning could take too long to be effective, or could be wrongly directed.

Effective learning plus effective resources equal effective outcomes and training is the means by which a systematic process is directed at improving performance, through organized learning, to produce effective outcomes.

As trainers, whether full-time or part-time, in-house, line managers or consultants we are convinced that training is an investment that is cost-effective and necessary to the long term success of the organization, so why do many boards of directors and senior managers not share the same view? Why is training seen as a cost instead of an investment?

A report produced in 1985 by Coopers and Lybrand, as a result of a study to examine the attitudes of British management compared to their European counterparts, refers to investment in vocational education and training. Some of their findings relating to British attitudes to investment in training are:

- Expenditure on training is rarely seen or treated as an investment in any financial sense.
- Decisions on training expenditure tend to be made at the manager level rather than at chief executive level.
- When decisions are made they tend to be reactive rather than proactive.
- Training expenditure is seen as an overhead that can be reduced when times are hard rather than as an investment leading to improved competitiveness.

Compare this with the German management attitude where business recession is seen not only as an opportunity to train for the future, but as a necessity in order to meet continued challenges.

One of the major challenges facing organizations, not only in the UK but also in many other countries throughout the world, is the need to recognize the relationship between systematically applied training and profitability. In an attempt to promote this in the UK the Department of Employment, since 1987, has embarked on an Annual National Award Programme in its quest to raise the awareness of organizations to the necessity of investing in training. It states:

*Training is a business activity. Its objectives are serious and it requires serious management. Training exists to support the business. The business does not exist to support training. So, inevitably, training is the responsibility of business leaders, not just personnel specialists. When it receives proper attention from top management it can assist the strategic development of the business, improve operational performance and help to cope with contingencies.*

*Employment Department(1992)*

A more recent initiative in the UK is the Employment Department Investors in People award. In order to qualify for the award the organization needs to demonstrate commitment to continuous personal development of its human resources. (Now see the Activity box.)

## ACTIVITY

What is your organization's attitude towards training? Does the attitude of non-training managers differ from that of trainers in the organization? What evidence do you have to support this view?

There are a number of issues which have been identified as being important to small and medium-sized organizations:

- profitability;
- marketing/increasing sales;

- cash flow;
- cost reduction/containment;
- stock control/inventory;
- improving productivity;
- competition from both UK and abroad.

These issues, in similar ranking order, broadly approximate to those identified in larger organizations.

This information is of direct relevance to you as a trainer because for your role to be effective your interventions need to address the major issues affecting your organization. You need to be able to provide evidence that you are attending to some of those issues.

For your training to be seen as relevant, and therefore as an investment, you must be able to establish strong links between the identified problem, the aim of the training, the likely costs of the intervention and the identified outcomes in terms of performance improvement. The stronger the identified links between training and the organization's performance, the stronger and more credible your continued requests for investment in training.

Performance problems and training investment are not simply confined to private or production oriented organizations, however. Public sector or service providers are equally vulnerable.

It may be more difficult, in a service-based organization, to identify specifically where performance problems are likely to occur. This is further complicated by what we see as problems. In many instances, what is perceived as a performance problem may be only a symptom of something happening elsewhere in the organization. Take the following example:

A large brewing organization, with many interlinking departments (including its tenanted public houses) reported a series of performance problems to the training manager. These problems included a high number of clerical errors, complaints to and from the public house managers about data received, increased levels of absenteeism and poor financial accountability and support.

At first sight it looked as if some support training was needed for the clerical staff to improve their error record and some training for pub managers to reinforce the need for accurate data reporting in the acceptable company format.

What was the response of the training manager?

After investigating the various problems, a week-long residential team-building and leadership intervention was developed for all of the involved departmental managers.

This was not such a crazy response when it becomes known that the performance problems identified earlier were simply symptoms of the very poor communication process between the departments. Each department had become so wrapped up in its own function that it had become its own reason for existence. Once the managers began to realize that they were all working for the same organization, and the sum of the contributions of the different, integrated departments were greater than the individual contributions of those departments, the performance problems (symptoms) began to disappear.

---

**ACTIVITY**

What performance problems can you identify within your organization that may actually have a cause other than the symptom?

---

Identifying causes rather than symptoms can often be quite difficult, especially if the 'problem' is presented to us by someone more senior in the organization. Below is a list of possibilities that could exist in your organization.

- high staff turnover;
- poor retention rates for new staff;
- ineffective management of meetings;
- impact of new technology;
- few standardized procedures;
- no clearly identified performance standards;
- poorly identified objectives;
- distance between management and staff;
- poor communication, upwards, downwards and/or sideways;
- unclear decision-making process;
- lack of teamwork and co-operation, inter- and intra-departmental;
- inconsistent workload allocation;
- heavy workloads affecting the service provided;
- high level of customer complaints;
- indecisive management;
- poor organizational planning;
- lack of cover during staff absence;
- lack of follow-through after staff changes;
- long lead-time to take up of new ideas.

An organization's training investment should therefore be directed towards solving, or helping to solve, real or anticipated performance problems. Only if this is happening can training investment be justified, but one of the biggest barriers to this is often the organization's culture.

The organization's culture often sees training in terms of courses to be run, and identifying the 'right' people for those courses, rather than seeing training as a means of solving specific performance problems and improving performance. Until this shift in perception occurs then, as a trainer, your role may be limited to simply that of provider.

## WHOM DOES TRAINING BENEFIT?

The potential justifications for training include:

- increased output;
- fewer accidents;
- improved quality;
- less waste;
- reduced costs;
- reduced staff turnover;
- increased retention of new staff;
- improved motivation;
- more effective use of human resources;
- more effective use of other resources;
- improved service;
- ability to take more responsibility for own performance;
- more clearly identified career opportunities.

Some of these justifications appear to benefit the organization while others benefit the individual. In reality, however, the systematic training process benefits both the organization and the individual. This is because the relationship between the needs of the individual, the needs of the organization, and the identified training intervention is an extremely complex one. As a result of this relationship all parties benefit to a greater or lesser extent. It is simply a matter of degree.

The benefits, individual and organizational, of investing in training include the following:

### Improved customer satisfaction

Customers are a useful barometer for measuring successful performance. They are usually aware of a poorly trained workforce and may take their custom elsewhere.

### Lower staff turnover

Training and development can often improve staff motivation and commitment. It can also reflect positively on the external image of the organization therefore encouraging high calibre staff to join, and remain with, the organization.

### More effective deployment of staff

As training and development helps groups and individuals to become more flexible and competent across a range of tasks, the opportunities open to individuals within the organization increase, while the organization benefits from the flexibility of its workforce.

## More effective use of other resources

After investing, often heavily, in capital resources, training and development can enable individuals to adapt to changes in processes and procedures with little trauma. This enables the new system or equipment to become effective much more quickly.

## Improved performance

This is often reflected in higher customer satisfaction rates, better quality ratings, improved safety records, etc, and benefits the individual as much as the organization.

---

### ACTIVITY

Taking a recent training intervention you have been involved in, identify the benefits (a) to the organization, and (b) to the individual.

---

## SUMMARY

This chapter has covered a range of knowledge required to underpin your competence as a trainer and developer.

You should now be able confidently to identify the culture and structure of your organization as well as knowing where the training function 'fits' within it. This knowledge will be to your advantage when promoting the training function within your organization.

Having examined the culture and structure, you were introduced to the systematic training cycle and how it allowed the investment in training to be justified. This is particularly important at a time when many training budgets are being cut. You were then asked to identify your organization's reasons for investing in training and to identify symptoms and possible causes of performance problems. Once you had identified the performance problems you were able to identify the benefits of a systematic approach to training for both the organization and the individual.

This chapter has therefore given you an overview of training in the context of your organization. This is of vital importance; for simply to look at training as something that happens in a vacuum will lead to a stressed trainer, not a competent trainer.

## References

Coopers and Lybrand Associates (1985) *A Challenge to Complacency*, MSC/NEDO.

Department of Employment (1992) *National Training Awards Prospectus*, HMSO, London.

Handy, C B (1993) *Understanding Organizations*, third edition, Penguin, London.

## Further useful reading

Anderson, A H (1993) *Successful Training Practice: A Manager's Guide to Personnel Development*, Blackwell, Oxford. (Identifies how a co-operative approach between training specialists and managers can lead to a more effective, systematic approach to training.)

Buckley, R and Caple, J (1994) *The Theory and Practice of Training*, third edition, Kogan Page, London.

If you want to know more about organizational structures, see the following two books:

Cushway, B and Lodge, D (1993) *Organizational Behaviour and Design*, Kogan Page, London.

Huczynski, A and Buchanan, D (1991) *Organizational Behaviour*, second edition, Prentice Hall, London.

Moss, G (1993) *The Trainer's Desk Reference*, second edition, Kogan Page, London.

# 3

# The role of the trainer

## INTRODUCTION

Your role as a trainer within your organization will depend on several factors. They include the size and objectives of the organization, any problems or changes current or imminent, any training policies or training strategies adopted by it, the current status of the training function within the organization, your skills, knowledge and experience, and the overall culture of the organization. The primary focus of this chapter is on the different roles played by trainers and the most common tasks encountered as a result of those roles.

## IDENTIFYING APPROPRIATE ROLES

The Training and Development Lead Body (TDLB) occupational standards for trainers identify four major spheres of activity for trainers and developers:

**AREA A**   Identify training and development needs.
**AREA B**   Design training and development strategies and plans.
**AREA C**   Provide learning opportunities, resources and support.
**AREA D**   Evaluate the effectiveness of training and development.

In chapter 2 (p. 31) you will see that these four areas of activity relate directly to the training cycle. However, the emergence of competence-based training and development has had a significant impact on the roles trainers may now have to undertake.

### Training for competence

Until recently training tasks could be easily categorized. Your main task was probably to design and deliver training programmes to groups of people. There were a number of things taken for granted, for example:

- everyone was roughly at the same stage of development or skill;
- the course or programme would last for a set length of time;
- the trainer was responsible for 'setting the pace';

- learners had very little responsibility for their learning: they were 'taught';
- levels of knowledge were verified by tests or examinations;
- candidates were selected without the involvement of the trainer;
- every learner was subjected to the same learning experiences.

As a result training was standardized, everyone got the same product regardless of their own development needs. This could be highly successful for some kinds of development, for example, training for the introduction of a new computer software package where no one has previous experience. Although even this is not perfect as it does not take into consideration the different learning styles and speeds of individuals.

The following case study is an example of how training for competence can lead to extreme dissatisfaction when traditional approaches are used.

A colleague and I attended a three-day assessor and verifier training programme. It was an open programme with twelve delegates from different organizations around the UK. The objectives of the programme were clearly indicated in the promotional material and the outcome was to be competent to go away and develop a portfolio to satisfy the occupational standards for assessors and then to present the portfolio for assessment. As my colleague and I wanted to become accredited assessors this seemed an ideal developmental opportunity even though the cost was substantial.

Unfortunately, the event was a disaster in terms of my development and that of one or two others. Some of the delegates had come along to try to get a basic understanding of NVQs, some were misinformed, and others were there to gather information for their own organizations before they decided whether or not to get involved. The facilitators were relatively inexperienced and concentrated on trying to get everyone to the same level of knowledge and understanding which meant abandoning most of the pre-set objectives. Unfortunately that was at a level below that which three of us were already at. The feedback from all delegates, however, was unanimous in that no one was satisfied with the outcome of the three days.

This case clearly illustrates the differences, and potential difficulties, of developing learners for competence-based awards. Training and development for competence requires a rethink of many of the traditional training approaches and their tasks. It can provide opportunities for innovation in development (see the Activity box opposite).

Below is a description of some of the additional tasks required for effective competence-based training and development:

- defining learner's current competence;
- agreeing short-term learning priorities;
- agreeing learning objectives;
- agreeing learning plans and processes to monitor learning outcomes;

---

## ACTIVITY

Using your knowledge of traditional and competence-based development, identify the additional tasks that you might be required to carry out as a trainer and developer in a competence-based system.

---

- identifying appropriate learning strategies;
- providing collaborative learning opportunities;
- supporting the achievement of individuals' learning objectives;
- assisting and supporting the application of learning;
- evaluating the achievement of individual and group outcomes against objectives;
- modifying and adapting learning plans.

As you can see, the focus is very much on working with the individual. This does not mean the demise of group work – on the contrary, it remains an effective means of developing individuals. What is different, however, is the focus on individual development and achievement, that is, the needs of the individual over the needs of the group.

Depending on your organization's structure, culture, and priorities you are likely to spend varying amounts of time across the four key areas and the tasks identified above and you may also spend time on tasks that have not been identified here. As a trainer, however, your role should be focused on the four main spheres of activity.

As you develop as a trainer your role may become more specialized. You may concentrate on specific aspects of training and development, for example, design and delivery or supporting open learning. Conversely, your role may become more generalist, involving you in all aspects of training and development.

The other important factor, of course, is your own progression as a trainer. Your ambition may be to manage the training function or to have your own training consultancy. In terms of managing the training function, the skills and knowledge required are covered in depth in chapters 7 and 8 (pp. 125–75). Specific attention is given to consulting in chapter 8. However, to be an effective training manager or consultant all the material covered in this book is relevant to your underpinning development (see the Activity box).

It is unlikely that everything you do in a typical week fits neatly into the four areas and their sub-areas. For one thing, the administration that training seems to generate, the phone calls, the photocopying, the keeping up to date with what is going on in the rest of the organization, etc, all take time that we often feel could be more valuably spent elsewhere.

What you can begin to do now, however, is monitor how you spend your time and plan to spend it as effectively as you can. Alongside this you can begin to identify your own development needs as outlined in

## ACTIVITY

- Consider the activities outlined above.
- What tasks do you perform?
- Do all the activities you undertake fit into the four main areas identified?
- Are there any that do not seem to fit?
- How can you make your role more effective?
- Is there anything you need to start doing or stop doing?

chapter 1 (p. 11). Plan to assess and review your performance at least once a month.

The four major spheres of training and development activity were identified on p. 43. Each sphere is covered in depth in later chapters: training needs in chapter 6 (p. 101); strategies and plans in chapters 4 (p. 62) and chapter 7 (p. 125); learning provision and support in chapter 5 (p. 80); and evaluation in chapter 9 (p. 177). This next section therefore is going to concentrate on the specific tasks identified earlier in this chapter.

## TRAINING AND DEVELOPMENT TASKS

Competence- or outcome-based training requires an additional set of skills to that of training delivered traditionally on courses. This does not mean that course-based programmes are defunct; on the contrary, they are complementary to the competence-based development process. How the process differs from traditional training and development was explored in chapter 1 (p. 12). The emphasis is very much on the development of the individual but that is not at the expense of group working. It simply means that group working is more specifically targeted to meet the outcomes required by the *individuals* and that they may differ from individual to individual. Each of those supporting activities was identified earlier in the chapter; here they are explored in more detail.

### Defining learner's current competence

There are a number of ways in which you can assist in this process:

- providing information;
- providing resources;
- accessing information;
- facilitating.

This is illustrated in Figure 3.1.

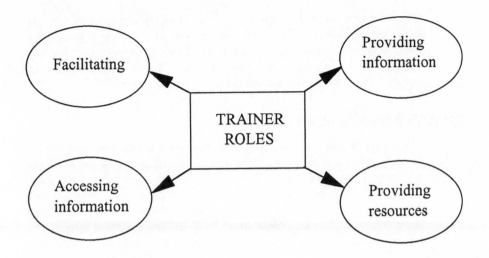

**Figure 3.1** *Defining learner's current competence*

### Providing information

This will usually consist of identifying the relevant performance standards from either national occupational standards or from organizationally derived standards. You will need therefore to be familiar with current standards of performance and be able to access and interpret them where necessary. There are two main groups of people that will require this information; the learners and their managers. It is essential that line managers have access to this information as it is they who are familiar with individual performance and can provide you with relevant feedback.

### Providing resources

Again, this will be to both learners and their managers. The resources could include your skill and knowledge of a particular functional area, internally or externally devised checklists against which current performance can be identified, along with the opportunities to demonstrate competence. It may also include methods for assessing evidence of current knowledge.

### Accessing information

There are a number of ways you can access information about an individual's current competence. A discussion with their line manager, appraisal records, assessment reports and internally designed records of their performance, or skill matrices, for example, continuous development plans, can all provide you with a relatively current written record of the individual's current competence.

### Facilitating

You are the catalyst in the process. By bringing together individuals and knowledge you can assist individuals to identify their own competence.

You can supplement this with the observations of others to enable you to gain an accurate picture of the individual's starting point for development. This is vital in order to allow the opportunity for the accreditation of prior learning and experience. It is also less wasteful of resources as learners are not forced to 'cover old ground'.

## Identifying learning objectives

Once current competence has been established it becomes possible to identify appropriate learning objectives. There are a number of methods you can use to assist in this process. They include counselling, accessing the advice of experts, reference to business plans and priorities and coaching. By using a combination of these methods you can effectively facilitate the identification of the individual's learning objectives. Once their learning objectives have been identified they will need to be prioritized.

## Agreeing short-term learning priorities

Identifying short-term priorities will require you to take a number of factors into consideration. To do this it will be necessary to access information on current business needs and also the current role of the individual. As an NVQ is made up of many units it is possible to identify which ones are most relevant at the current time for both the individual and the organization. Similarly, with organizationally devised standards the most appropriate interpersonal, process or functional skills units can be identified. By a process of negotiation it is possible to identify objectives that meet the short-term needs of both the individual and the organization.

## Identifying appropriate learning strategies

Identifying appropriate learning strategies is of vital importance to the effective development of individuals and has been referred to several times already in this section on training and development tasks. Within a competence- or outcome-based system learners are given much more responsibility for their own learning and development and therefore they also have a greater responsibility for selecting appropriate learning strategies. The role of the trainer in this process is to act as facilitator or guide to help the individual identify the most appropriate learning strategies for them.

Factors that need to be considered include:

- outcomes required;
- resources available;
- preferred learning style;
- opportunities available within current job role;
- opportunities available within the organization;
- time-scale.

Learning design and the implications for learning outcomes is the focus of chapter 4 where learning styles are discussed in depth. What the above factors have in common is their effect on the development of the individual's learning plan.

## Agreeing learning plans and processes to monitor learning outcomes

Once learning objectives have been prioritized it is then possible to agree individual learning plans. A number of factors relating to learning will influence this, as Figure 3.2 shows.

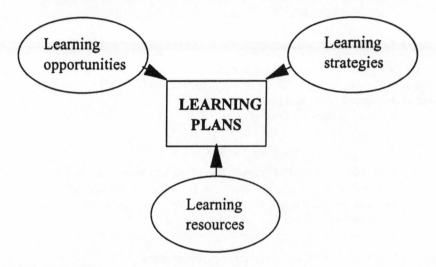

Figure 3.2 *Factors influencing learning plans*

### *Learning strategies*

The two major learning strategies are reflective learning and active learning. When negotiating the learning plan the most appropriate learning strategy can be selected depending on the learning objectives identified, the learner's preferred style and the learning opportunities that are available. See also page 48.

### *Learning opportunities*

Depending on the identified learning objectives these opportunities may be on-the-job, off-the-job, or a combination of both. The identification of learning opportunities is discussed in depth in chapter 5 (p. 80). In order to identify the most appropriate range of opportunities available you will need to consider opportunities that are or can be made available in the learner's current role, the outcomes required, for example, performance and/or knowledge development and the resources available.

### Learning resources

Learning resources include facilities, materials, equipment and personnel available. Identifying the most appropriate resources may, however be subject to a number of constraints (see the Activity box).

## ACTIVITY

What constraints may there be affecting your selection of the most appropriate learning resources to meet the objectives specified in the learning plan?

Constraints could include:

- the 'expert' not being available;
- room not suitable for the activities required;
- not enough equipment;
- not the right sort of equipment;
- no suitable simulation available;
- no suitable work experience available.

You will often have to negotiate and compromise in order to achieve a learning plan that is achievable. The learning plan should include what is to be achieved, using what method(s), with what resources, when it is to be reviewed and when it is to be assessed.

## Providing collaborative learning opportunities

We saw on p. 45 that the focus on the individual in a competence- or outcome-based approach to development did not mean the demise of group work. On the contrary, groups can be very effective vehicles for individual development providing that a number of criteria are met.

1. The outcomes required of the group are similar to the outcomes required by the individual members of that group.
2. The outcomes required of the group and its individual members are clearly defined at the start.
3. The exercise or simulation chosen is sufficiently realistic to allow the outcomes to be both valid and achievable.
4. The facilities, including the locations, equipment and materials are able to support group interaction.
5. The materials identified to support the exercise or simulation are appropriate, accurate and realistic.
6. There is appropriate and effective co-ordination of the activities.

These criteria will now be examined in more detail.

## 1. Individual and group outcomes

It is important when designing and using developmental methods with groups of people that the participants share similar developmental needs. Although this is an obvious statement, the case study on page 44 shows that it does not always happen. If, however, the processes identified so far under training and development tasks are followed, then it is possible for the trainer, and the individuals, to get a reasonably accurate picture of what those development needs are prior to group exercise, simulation or training intervention. Your role is to collate that information from the individual learning plans in order to identify who should be participating in what (see the Activity box).

---

### ACTIVITY

Answer the following questions:

1. How are individuals currently selected for a group exercise, simulation or training intervention in your organization?
2. How could this be improved?
3. What benefits would this have for the learners, the trainers and the organization?
4. What are the likely resource implications of those changes?

---

## 2. Clearly defined outcomes

This is vital if learners are to see the relevance of the exercise for their development. If outcomes are not clearly defined from the start how can the learners identify whether what they are doing is appropriate and how can you and the learners identify when they have achieved them?

## 3. Realistic exercises and simulations

In order for the outcomes of a simulation or exercise to be valid for assessment purposes any exercise or simulation must match normal performance conditions as closely as is realistically possible. It may be impossible in many situations to exactly replicate the normal performance environment but great attention to detail must be paid in the setting up of exercises to protect their assessment integrity and validity. In terms of outcome- or competence-based assessment it is therefore important that the performance criteria and range statement conditions are met. You will therefore need to study them closely when designing the exercise or simulation.

## 4. Appropriate facilities

Facilities include locations, equipment and materials. The facilities will depend on the types of groups needed for the exercise or simulation.

Types of groups include:

- task or production;
- problem-solving;
- discussion;
- small (4-8 members);
- medium-sized (up to 30 members), with or without syndicates (see text below);
- large (over 30 members), with or without syndicates (see text below);
- stable (group composition always stays the same);
- mixed (group composition differs from task to task).

Obviously group size and whether or not you are going to use syndicate groups, ie, smaller sub-groups within the main group, will affect the type of location you need, as will the task itself.

The equipment you require will also be determined by the exercise or simulation and this is covered in more detail in chapter 5 (p. 88). Appropriate materials are discussed below.

## 5. Appropriate materials

Apart from the obvious criterion of ensuring that there are sufficient materials to meet the needs of the learners, there are a number of other criteria that need to be accommodated:

- the functions of the materials;
- their relevance and credibility;
- the format of the materials;
- their cost;
- their currency.

### ACTIVITY

What kind of functions could learning materials fulfil?

Learning materials could be used to:

- identify learning;
- give instructions;
- evaluate progress;
- stimulate discussion;
- provide good practice;
- provide practical experience;

- provide information;
- facilitate group working.

Learning materials are also discussed in more depth in chapter 5 (p. 89).

## 6. Effective co-ordination

Without effective co-ordination group exercises and activities can fail to produce the required outcomes. Your role will include facilitating group discussion, providing information on progress when requested, providing clarification where necessary and assessing and evaluating the outcomes of the exercise or simulation and feeding this back effectively to the participants. By facilitating these processes you will be enhancing the opportunities that the individuals have for learning. There are a range of processes that you can use to enhance your effectiveness. You can:

- provide summaries and reviews of your observations of group and individuals' activities and performance;
- use appropriate questioning to ascertain understanding and achievement;
- challenge or confront the group or individuals within it to stimulate reflection or to question values or beliefs;
- seek agreement or consensus from the group on thoughts or actions.

By using this combination of skills you can encourage the group, and the individuals within it, to achieve the desired outcomes. As with all groups, individuals can be expected to develop at different rates and in different ways. By providing support to individuals on the achievement of their learning objectives, whether as part of a group situation or on individual performance, you will ensure that no one gets 'left behind'.

## Supporting the achievement of an individual's learning objectives

Outcome- or competence-based development and assessment can result in a greater demand for individual support and feedback than with work for traditional qualifications. It is paradoxical that a system that relies much more on learner-centred approaches, with the emphasis on the ownership of learning by the individual, can also make greater demands, at least in the early stages, on the trainer (see the Activity box).

## ACTIVITY

What processes can you use to help support learners in achieving their learning objectives?

You can:

1. Provide information and advice.
2. Provide learning opportunities.
3. Provide opportunities to review and modify learning objectives.
4. Collate and use information on the progress of individual learners.

## 1. Provide information and advice

This is a particularly important aspect when providing support to learners, especially during the early stages of development. As learners become more adept they should be encouraged to be proactive in seeking advice whereas during the early stages of a development programme it is likely that they will be more dependent on you to provide this service almost as a 'mind reader'.

The key issues at stake here are your understanding of the different types of learner and learning styles, the types of learning opportunities that are available and their relevance to the learning objectives and your ability to give feedback in a way that promotes learning. This is illustrated in Figure 3.3.

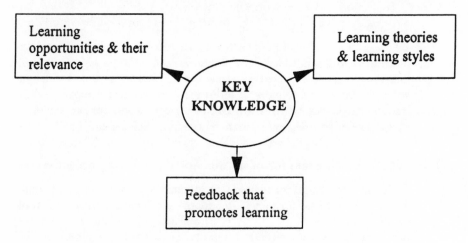

**Figure 3.3** *Supporting learner achievement*

Learning theories and learning styles are discussed in more detail in chapter 4 (p. 62), learning opportunities and their relevance are discussed in chapter 5 (p. 80), and feedback skills are the subject of the final section of this chapter (p. 57).

## 2. Provide learning opportunities

Learning outcomes are covered in detail in chapter 4 (p. 75) and learning opportunities in chapter 5 (p. 80). The main factors to be considered are to:

- identify those opportunities that have the greatest chance of success;

- avoid disadvantaging learners by the selection of inappropriate opportunities;
- ensure that where the opportunities are to be provided externally, the providers are given accurate and detailed learning and performance outcomes.

## 3. Provide opportunities to review and modify learning objectives

There are a number of ways in which you can enable the learner to identify appropriate review opportunities. You can include formal and informal review sessions within the training intervention. This could include:

- peer review;
- self-assessment and review;
- formal assessment by the trainer;
- informal feedback by the trainer.

You could also use opportunities that are external to the formal training intervention by encouraging the involvement of the line manager in the review process. If the learner has access to a counsellor, mentor or coach they should be receiving feedback from these sources to enable them to review their progress so far against their identified learning objectives. This is particularly useful when considering the continuing relevance of previously identified learning outcomes, since job roles, tasks and therefore learning opportunities, may change over time.

## 4. Collate and use information on the progress of individual learners

This is necessary to enable you to give valid feedback and guidance to learners on their progress towards their learning and performance objectives. The types of information you can use include:

- assessment records;
- feedback from line managers;
- feedback from learners about any:
  - difficulties they are encountering
  - relevant personal circumstances.

You will need to summarize all this information accurately and inform learners of their rights of access to this information. Ideally learners should have complete freedom of access to information that is held about their progress but not all organizations share this view. You will therefore have to acquaint yourself with your organization's policy on this issue and inform learners accordingly. It is, of course, vital that this information is stored securely so that only those who have a right to it can access it. Again, the systems for doing this may differ from organization to organization but the confidentiality of the learners' records must be guaranteed.

## Assisting and supporting the application of learning

This is dealt with in chapter 5 (p. 96) under the heading of 'transferring learning'.

## Evaluating the achievement of individual and group outcomes against objectives

Evaluation is discussed in depth in chapter 9 (p. 177). The key features of this process are:

- choosing valid and appropriate methods;
- obtaining additional information, where required, from other sources, eg, line managers;
- using a range of evidence types, including:
  - witness testimony
  - personal testimony
  - knowledge evidence
  - naturally occurring performance
  - simulated performance
  - appraisal or similar performance review

Methods for gathering information are discussed in chapter 8 (p. 171) and forms of assessment and acceptable evidence in chapter 10 (p. 196).

## Modifying and adapting learning plans

All the above processes can lead to the modification of existing learning plans. This may result in a change to only part of a plan, but could mean revising the whole plan, depending on the circumstances. Even where it is just a short-term learning plan, circumstances can change which render it inappropriate to the learner's needs. If you have followed the processes outlined above then you will be in a position to intervene, with appropriate information, and, at the appropriate time, to facilitate this with the learner.

The criteria for modification are the same as the criteria for agreeing a learning plan, except that you are making modifications with much more information about the learner. This should make the process easier for all concerned. It may be as simple as working towards a different unit of an NVQ or it may mean changing the level of NVQ or even changing to a different NVQ altogether. The same applies, of course, to any other type of standards or qualification used as a basis for the training intervention. Figure 3.4 illustrates how the training and development tasks discussed in this section contribute to and facilitate the development of the learner.

As you can see from the above, one of the major skills common to all the tasks is feedback, both giving and receiving it. This skill is of vital importance if your intervention and support is to be effective for both you and the learner. The final section of this chapter therefore explores in some depth the skills of giving and receiving feedback.

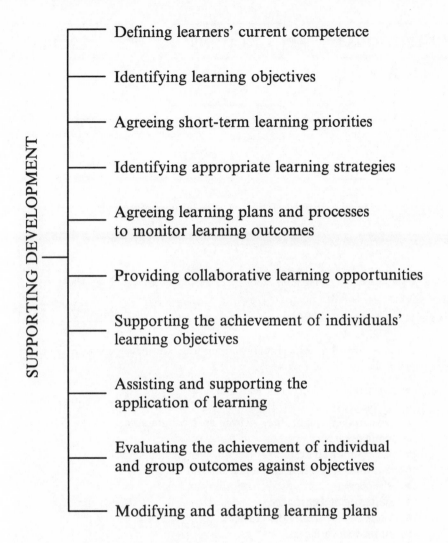

**Figure 3.4** *Supporting learner development*

## GIVING AND RECEIVING FEEDBACK

Feedback is a constant factor in our lives. Whether it is the unexpected reflection in a shop window, someone's non-verbal response to us or an actual comment on our behaviour, feedback causes us to think about ourselves. When we initiate feedback, either in giving or inviting it, we are in the business of behaviour change which, if it is to be successful, requires a willingness to accommodate, understand and adapt as a result. The feedback loop is represented in Figure 3.5 (see also the Activity box).

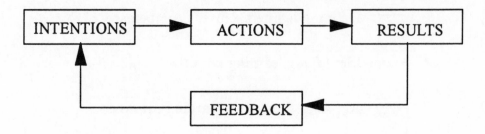

**Figure 3.5** *The feedback loop*

## ACTIVITY

Identify to whom you might be required to give feedback and from whom you might receive feedback.

Your Activity box lists should be identical. You have probably identified some or all of the following:

- students, candidates or learners;
- colleagues;
- 'experts' (brought in to deliver on a programme);
- your manager;
- your subordinates;
- customers, internal and external;
- suppliers;
- departmental managers;
- executive board of directors;
- individual directors;
- department heads;
- team members.

This list is not exclusive but covers most of the people you are required to provide feedback to or can expect to receive feedback from during your working day.

### Giving feedback

The most important guideline when providing feedback is to deal only with what you can see. You can only comment on what you can see as you do not know what the individual's intentions were, that is, what led them to take that particular action. This limits your conversations to actions and their results, in other words, what you were able to observe.

The following guidelines may help you improve your feedback skills:

1. Feedback is better when solicited rather than when imposed. It works best when the receiver has asked for it to be given.
2. Consider the timing. In general, feedback is most useful at the earliest opportunity after the given behaviour (depending, of course, on the person's readiness to hear it, on support available from others, etc).
3. Be descriptive rather than evaluative. Describing what we actually hear and see reduces the need for the other person to react in a defensive way.
4. Reveal your own position or feelings vis-à-vis the other persons. For example: 'I find it very frustrating when you turn up late to meetings.'
5. Be specific rather than general. To be told that one is disorganized will probably not be as useful as to be told: 'When you were asked to produce the report on assessment you left it to the last minute and it wasn't very convenient.'
6. Take into account the receiver's needs as well as your own. Feedback can be destructive when it serves only our needs and fails to consider the needs of the person on the receiving end.
7. Direct it towards behaviour that the receiver can control.
8. Check to ensure clear communication. One way of doing this is to have the receiver try to rephrase the feedback s/he has received to see if it corresponds to your understanding of what you have just said.
9. When feedback is given in a group, allow giver and receiver the opportunity to check the accuracy of the feedback with others in the group.

Those are the main skills of feedback and for giving positive feedback they are quite straightforward. Simply describe the actions and results in a straightforward way and add your comments on the achievement. When giving negative feedback you might find the following sequence effective:

1. Describe the actions you observed and their results.
2. Ask the individual if those were his/her intended results.
3. With a typical 'No' response ask what their intended results were.
4. Then ask what they could have done differently to achieve their desired results.
5. Identify any possible barriers to 'doing things differently', ie, lack of skills or resources.
6. Discuss any alternative course of action.
7. Agree a way to handle future, similar situations.
8. Conclude by summarizing the main points discussed and the actions agreed.

## Receiving feedback

Receiving feedback requires effective listening skills. Listening is often seen to be a passive process but effective listening requires you to give active attention to what is being said. You need to make sure that you are ready to listen and are not just paying lip-service to asking for feedback. It helps if you remember that feedback is given to help you learn and develop. It is not intended as personal criticism. The following guidelines may help:

1. Listen to the other's feedback – try to understand their feelings, what they are describing, what they suggest you do and their reasons for giving you feedback.
2. Give the feedback serious consideration; weigh up the consequences of changing/not changing, express thoughts and feelings about alternatives.
3. Communicate any decision made as a result of the feedback to the person/s who gave you the feedback.
4. Tell others what s/he or they could do which might help you to change.
5. Express appreciation of the other's concern. Thank the feedback giver and tell him/her what specific information you have found useful.

---

## ACTIVITY

Earlier you were asked to identify to *whom* or *from whom* you might give or receive feedback. Now you are asked to identify *when* you are required to give or receive feedback.

---

Here are a few examples of answers to the Activity exercise:

- during an exercise or simulation;
- after assessment;
- as part of a review session;
- at the end of a training intervention;
- at the end of an exercise or simulation;
- when reviewing learning objectives;
- when reviewing a learning plan;
- when summarizing learner achievement.

## SUMMARY

This chapter has covered a wide range of information necessary to increase your knowledge about the role of the trainer within an organization or as a consultant to organizations. It began by identifying the four major spheres of activity for trainers and you were asked to quantify and monitor your day-to-day performance. The additional tasks facing trainers and consultants involved in outcome- or competence-based training were then identified and explored in detail. Where appropriate links were made to other chapters where issues raised by these changes are discussed in more detail.

One of the major skills identified as essential as a result of this analysis was that of giving and receiving feedback and the final section of the chapter focused on developing effective feedback knowledge and skills in this area.

## Further useful reading

Buckley, R and Caple, J (1991) *One-to-one Training and Coaching Skills*, Kogan Page, London.

Cockman, P, Evans, B and Reynolds, P (1994) *Client-centred Consulting: A Practical Guide for Internal Advisors and Trainers*, McGraw Hill, London.

Phillips, K and Shaw, P (1989) *A Consultancy Approach for Trainers*, Gower, Aldershot.

Pont, T (1990) *Developing Effective Training Skills*, McGraw Hill, London.

Rae, L (1993) *The Skills of Training: A Guide for Managers and Practitioners*, second edition, Gower, Aldershot.

Russell, T (1994) *Effective Feedback Skills*, Kogan Page, London.

Saunders, M and Holdaway, K (1992) *The In-house Trainer as Consultant*, Kogan Page, London.

# 4

# Learning design and learning outcomes

## INTRODUCTION

The role of the trainer seems, on the one hand, to be a very straightforward and simple one. We train people. On the other hand, if we analyse what we are doing while we are 'training' people, we find it is not perhaps as straightforward as first surmised. If we are working effectively as trainers we are not training people or teaching people, we are helping people to learn.

The essence of training therefore is to help learners learn, to help people develop. Trainers cannot teach anyone anything – we can only facilitate their learning. Learning is a complex phenomenon, however, with many interacting factors.

This chapter identifies the key issues of learning by considering the many factors that can influence the success, or otherwise, of your intervention.

Before you can begin to design or develop a training intervention to address a performance problem you need to identify the factors that are likely to affect the success of the intervention in terms of its being a successful learning opportunity for the participant/s.

The *Glossary of Training Terms* (Manpower Services Commission 1981) defines training and learning as:

### Training

*A planned process to modify attitude, knowledge or skill behaviour through learning experience to achieve effective performance in an activity or range of activities. Its purpose, in the work situation, is to develop the abilities of the individual and to satisfy the current and future manpower needs of the organization.*

### Learning

*The process whereby individuals acquire knowledge, skills and attitudes through experience, reflection, study or instruction.*

Everyone is capable of learning. We begin to learn as soon as we are born and yet how many times have you heard people say 'I can't, I was no good at school and I'll never be able to learn anything.' They have a misperception about their abilities and their capacity to learn and yet they are learning new things all the time. It is just that they have been programmed to see learning as something that comes from books, something formal. If we were not able to learn or develop new skills then we would be poor, helpless creatures dependent on external means to exist. We would be just like a newborn baby with purely physiological reflexes (see the Activity box).

## ACTIVITY

List all the things you had learned to do by the time you started school.

In doing the Activity exercise you may have included some or all of the following:

- crawl
- walk
- feed yourself
- tie your shoelaces
- control your bladder
- control your bowels
- ride a bike
- get dressed
- clean your teeth

- knives are sharp
- fire burns
- it hurts when you fall down
- nursery rhymes
- ice cream tastes nice
- talk
- cuddles feel good
- don't talk to strangers
- your address

## FOUR LEARNING STRATEGIES

The way you learned the items in your list can be identified from the following four categories:

1. Trial and error.
2. Being told or instructed.
3. Copying or imitating someone else.
4. Thinking for yourself.

## ACTIVITY

Go back to your original list, adding any other things you have remembered, and identify against each one the type/s of learning you used to learn each item.

One of the problems we face as trainers is deciding how best to help someone learn. This will depend on the task or skill to be learned, the resources available (including time and cost), as well as the existing knowledge held by the individual and their preferred learning style. This becomes even more complex when you are providing learning opportunities for a group of people, as all may have different existing skill or knowledge bases and different preferred learning styles.

On p. 63 the four major ways you can learn were identified: We can now consider them in more detail. It is important to remember, however, that we normally use more than one of the four methods, in differing combinations of emphasis, depending on the task or skill to be learned. For example, when learning to tie your shoelaces it is likely that you were shown how to do it, tried it for yourself, made mistakes, tried again, thought about why it didn't work properly, tried or were shown again and then finally got it right with practice.

## 1. Trial and error

This is essentially a practical activity and is the most traditional form of learning. Learners often refer to it as 'having-a-go'. One of the most important aspects of this type of learning is known as 'knowledge of results'. We more commonly refer to this as feedback. All the opportunities to 'have-a-go' in the world will be valueless unless we know whether or not we have been successful. The feedback confirms if the attempt has been successful and often indicates the reasons for its success or failure.

As a trainer, you need to ensure that any learning event you design which is based on this strategy allows the learner to successfully achieve a positive outcome and therefore provides positive reinforcement of acceptable performance. You also need to be able to provide verbal feedback to support this development in the event of unsuccessful performance. Giving feedback was covered in detail in chapter 3 (p. 43). If this is properly planned then trial and error learning can be a valuable strategy when it is incorporated into a training plan to correct a performance problem. It is also a very useful strategy to adopt when carrying out on-the-job training.

## 2. Being told or instructed

Being told or given instructions can be a very prescriptive approach as it often requires the learner/s to be passive. It also puts the trainer in the role of 'expert' and this can become a barrier for some learners, maybe because they do not respond to authority figures reminiscent of their schooldays, or perhaps because they feel the knowledge and experience they already have is not being acknowledged.

This strategy rarely requires learners to find things out for themselves as the information you have determined they need is often all provided for them. This is quite a passive strategy, therefore, and relies upon the trainer being able to effectively pass on the body of knowledge required. It is often an essential stage in the acquisition of competence, however, as without the underpinning knowledge needed for some tasks competence cannot be attained.

## 3. Copying or imitating someone else

This strategy needs to be considered very carefully by the trainer, particularly where specific job-skills are being learned. Unless the trainer is also working on the 'shop-floor' or in an environment where standardization is not common there is the possibility that what is learned 'off-the-job' is different from the way it is performed 'on-the-job'. This can result in a negative perception of the usefulness of training and can erode the credibility of the training function.

Learning by imitation 'on-the-job', providing it is well structured and monitored, can be a very powerful learning strategy. This does depend on the demonstrator providing a positive demonstration of the skill or task, ie, the correct way to do something, otherwise you are simply passing on bad or even dangerous practices. Learners should not therefore be exposed to bad practices or poor models of behaviour. A good performance model should always be available so that the learner can imitate a positive model and the learner should be able to accurately observe the complete process, task or skill.

## 4. Thinking for yourself

This could also be called reflection. Learning occurs when you are encouraged to think about something that you have done, some skill you have attempted to demonstrate or some problem you have tried to solve. You are able to reflect on what went right, what went wrong and *why*.

As a trainer you can encourage this process by asking the learner certain questions like: 'Why did that happen?', 'What caused that?', 'How could you have done it differently?' Often there is not a single solution to a problem and you can encourage the learner to think through the options that are available to them. This process of evaluation, interpretation, consideration and reflection is particularly effective in a group setting where different options may be challenged by other learners.

One of the greatest difficulties for the trainer is trying to avoid imposing a personal or 'right' solution to the problem. This is essentially a learner-centred approach and is only effective when approached in an advisory way, with the trainer acting as counsellor or facilitator rather than as the 'expert'.

Identifying the major learning strategy used in the delivery of the intervention is often quite difficult, as we commonly use a mix of all four strategies in any one learning event or programme. There is usually a dominant strategy, however, and this can be determined by many factors. They are discussed in more detail later in this chapter.

As individual learners we also tend to develop a preferred style of learning and these styles match up closely with the four learning strategies identified above. They also relate very closely to what has been described by Kolb (1974) as the learning cycle.

## THE EXPERIENTIAL LEARNING CYCLE

This is a four-stage learning process and is the model often referred to to describe experiential learning (see Figure 4.1). The process can begin at any of the stages and is continuous, ie, there is no limit to the number of cycles you can make in a learning situation.

The key stages are experience, reflection, planning new behaviour and trying out that behaviour. Each of the stages is vital to successful learning. Without reflection we would simply continue to repeat our mistakes;

**Concrete Experience**
Putting it into practice

**Active Experimentation**
Experimentng to find solutions

**Reflective Observation**
Objectively analyse the outcome

**Abstract Conceptualization**
Reviewing your conceptual understanding

**Figure 4.1** *The experiential learning cycle*

without planning new behaviour we would be aware of our mistakes but not do anything about them; without putting the plan into operation we would never know whether our ideas would work. The whole process of experience, reflection, planning and implementation also reinforces our learning. It gives us a greater understanding of what we do and how and why we are doing it.

Each of the learning strategies we identified earlier only encompasses some of the stages in the cycle. It is because of this that effective learning events need to contain more than one strategy.

Thinking for yourself is only part of the cycle. Without concrete experience to base it on or opportunities for active experimentation you would not be able to test your conclusions. Imitating someone else allows you to gain concrete experience but you also need to be able to reflect on what you have done and to be able to plan and try out improvements or variations where the task allows. Being told or instructed can give you concrete experience but may not allow reflection or planning or transfer of the learning to new situations. Trial and error comes closest to following all the stages of the learning cycle but if it is unsupervised there is no guarantee that the application of the learning can be transferred to new environments or situations.

As trainers therefore we have a responsibility to ensure that the learner travels through all four stages of the learning cycle so that successful learning may take place. You might ask, 'What's the difference between learning and successful learning?' Surely if you learn something, that is success. But it is possible to demonstrate the difference on at least two levels.

Firstly, at the end of a learning event the learner may be fully convinced that they have learned something new or that they are now competent in a skill. For example, when we board an aircraft the stewardess takes us through the safety routine; how to fasten your seat belt, where the exits are, how to inflate your life-jacket, what to do if there is a loss of cabin pressure, etc.

We listen, or not, and then just sit back and get on with the flight. We fasten and unfasten our safety belts when we need to and think no more about what we have been told. In the ensuing panic of a mishap could we remember, and follow, the instructions we were given earlier? For most of us the answer is probably *no*. As a result of an incomplete learning experience we could therefore be a danger to ourselves and to others. This is not successful learning.

Secondly, if we are training 'off-the-job' the learner may successfully demonstrate a particular skill a number of times under simulated conditions. The trainer and the learner both view this as success. We have set out to improve or develop performance and here is the evidence that this has happened.

But what evidence do we have that this skill can be successfully performed under normal working conditions? Until we have evidence that the learner can successfully transfer their learning to the normal working environment then we cannot say that successful learning has taken place. This is essential when we begin to develop learners whose success will be measured against competence in the workplace and against measurable performance standards.

## Honey and Mumford's learning styles

There is also a link between the learning cycle and the way we prefer to learn. Most of us can identify the way in which we feel we learn best. Honey and Mumford (1986) identified four predominant learning styles that we can link in with the learning cycle and the four major strategies for learning. They are:

- activist;
- reflector;
- theorist;
- pragmatist.

### 1. Activist

This is the 'try anything once' style. You are likely to act first and ask questions or consider consequences only after your actions. You enjoy a challenge but once you have mastered a problem you become bored and want to move on to something new. You are usually open-minded and enthusiastic about new events or situations.

### 2. Reflector

This is the cautious style. You prefer to collect as much information as possible and study it thoroughly before coming to a conclusion. You consider all possible angles and all possible consequences before making a move. You enjoy observing and listening to others before contributing or acting. You hate being rushed and don't jump to conclusions.

### 3. Theorist

This is the logical style. You tend to be a perfectionist and enjoy pulling together seemingly unrelated pieces of information to make a coherent theory. You like to analyse information or situations and like working within a clear system. You tend to be rational and objective in the way you work and like things to 'make sense'. You like things to be certain and dislike subjectivity and light-hearted approaches to situations.

### 4. Pragmatist

This is the practical style. Problems are seen as challenges and you are keen to get on with things. You like to experiment with new ideas and enjoy putting new things into practice to see if they work. You enjoy making decisions and problem-solving but can get quite impatient with people who want to discuss things in more detail. You enjoy looking at ways to improve things.

Each of these styles has its strengths and weaknesses and although we usually have one style that dominates our learning we also have characteristics from the other three styles. This information is quite important when we are planning a learning event as it will have an impact on its effectiveness. By being aware of the strengths and weaknesses of the different learning styles we can also accommodate this into our working style. It is not uncommon for a trainer to favour one predominant style of delivery, when on further analysis this is identified as the trainer's preferred learning style!

We can become more effective learners ourselves, and encourage our learners to do likewise, by advocating the benefits of developing our less predominant styles. By doing this we will be producing more flexible learners who are able to make the most of any learning opportunity. Honey and Mumford (1986) explore this in much more depth in their book *Using Your Learning Styles*. Now see the Activity box.

## ACTIVITY

Using the information provided so far in this chapter, along with your own experience, list the questions you need to ask before you can begin to design a learning event.

In doing the Activity exercise you could have identified some or all of the following questions:

- What is the purpose of the event?
- What am I aiming to develop?
- Whom am I developing?
- What can they do already?
- Which strategy is most suitable for what I want the learners to develop?
- How can I ensure that all four stages in the learning cycle are covered?
- How can I ensure that the learner's learning style will enable them to benefit from the event?
- What is my role? Is it expert, adviser, facilitator?
- What are the consequences of the learner/s failing to learn successfully?

Also, there are other issues we need to consider when designing a learning event. They include:

- performance standards that are occupationally identified;
- the range of intervention methods we could use;
- the motivation and prior knowledge or experience of the learners;

- the opportunities available to the learners to transfer their learning and develop their competence.

These factors are considered in more detail later in this chapter. First, however, we need to identify a framework for producing a design brief.

## THE DESIGN BRIEF

So far we have looked at some of the key principles to be considered when we begin to design a learning event. However, the design process should begin with a clearly identified brief: in other words, a clearly shared understanding between you and your customer as to what is expected from the intervention.

Customer, in this context, has many interpretations. It could be the learner, a department manager, an external client or another member of your organization. Whoever it is, they are crucial to the development of the brief. It is therefore a partnership activity.

If you attempt to design a learning intervention without any consultation with the customer then you run the risk of producing at best something barely adequate and at worst something totally inappropriate. So while it is possible for you to work in isolation, relying solely on your understanding of the performance problem and all the other factors related to it, you will produce a much more realistic, practical and effective design if you negotiate and clarify the brief with the customer.

What exactly is a design brief? A working definition could be 'a clearly identified plan, developed in conjunction with a customer, to provide a training and development intervention to improve a performance problem, current or anticipated.'

Before you begin the design process there are a number of key issues to be decided (see Figure 4.2).

As these issues are decided the understanding between you and the customer will also become clearer. You will then be able to design an intervention that is practical and effective, that is within the resources available to you and that addresses effectively the identified performance problem. The issues include:

- The performance problem;
- The objectives of the intervention;
- The required outcomes;
- The resources available;
- The timescale involved;
- The learner/s likely entry behaviour.

These questions are particularly important when the customer may be misinformed, either about the cause of the problem or about possible solutions. This can be a problem in organizations where training has been seen simply as a reactive function as there is a reluctance to see the trainer

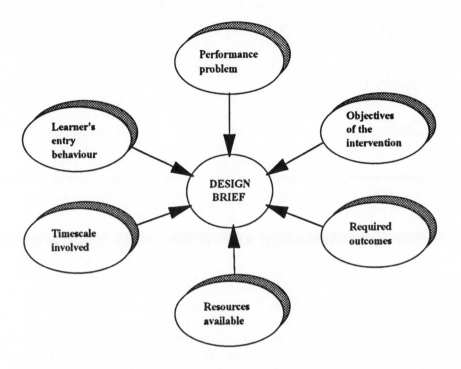

**Figure 4.2** *Influences on the design brief*

as an expert. This type of culture has historically relied on 'telling the training department what we want' (see the Activity box). The negotiation skills identified in chapter 8 (p. 168) may be particularly useful when this occurs.

---

## ACTIVITY

What problems might the customer telling you what they want cause for you as a trainer when attempting to design a training brief to address a performance problem?

---

A number of problems may arise for both you and the customer.

1. They may not have clearly or correctly identified the performance problem.
2. They may have identified a standard or inappropriate training solution.
3. They may have unrealistic expectations of the outcomes of any intervention.

4. A training intervention may not be the most appropriate solution to the problem.

And who gets the blame if it does not produce the results? That's right, you do! So let us look at the key factors of the design brief in more detail.

## The performance problem

The current or anticipated problem needs to be established and agreed. What is causing the problem and who it is affecting needs to be established. We shall examine this in more detail in chapter 6 (p. 101) when we look at training needs analysis and problem-solving. At this stage you also need to ascertain whether the problem requires a training intervention in terms of the individuals involved or whether it is a problem caused by the organization itself. If it is an organization problem then an intervention aimed at individuals is likely only to treat the symptoms and will not directly address the cause. You will therefore need to spend some time with the customer to identify and agree the problem.

## The objectives of the intervention

Learning a new skill, adapting an already acquired skill, eg as a result of new technology, changing behaviour or attitudes, updating knowledge or raising awareness are all legitimate objectives. What is not legitimate is manipulating someone's behaviour or attitudes to suit an organization's purpose if this is not done with the full knowledge and consent of the learner.

Ultimately the objective is to solve the performance problem, but for this to be effective it is necessary for you to analyse the problem and then decide with the customer which of the above are to be the focus of the intervention. This will also help to inform your choice of methods when you begin to plan the intervention in more detail.

## The required outcomes

Once you have identified the objectives of the intervention you will then be in a position to negotiate the required outcomes. This is the opportunity you have to identify in precise terms what your customer's expectations are from your intervention.

To negotiate a design brief without clarifying exactly what outcomes are required or expected can cause you many problems. It is not enough to simply conclude the brief with an overall definition of the performance problem as this does not ensure that your understanding of the problem matches that of the customer. Breaking the objectives down further into precise outcomes leaves little room for misunderstanding and ambiguity. Once the objectives are agreed and are in writing you can focus the intervention much more effectively. Also, breaking the objectives down into outcomes allows you to negotiate and correct any unrealistic expectations the customer has about what the intervention can accomplish.

### The resources available

You will need to clarify whether the intervention is to take place on-the-job or off-the-job. How much time do you anticipate you may need to achieve the agreed outcomes? Are you to be working on the customer's premises or at an off-site training centre? What budget do you have? What support do you expect from the customer and what support will they give the learner/s?

This last point is crucial. An intervention that relies wholly on the trainer to solve the problem is doomed. Without support and back-up from the learner's organization any learning that takes place is likely to be short-lived, even when the outcomes have been clearly identified. Again, negotiating the resources can help you correct any unrealistic expectations the customer may have about what is actually required to help ensure an effective solution to the problem.

### The timescale

Does the performance problem already exist? If so, does it require an immediate response? Beware of crisis planning and intervention! A training intervention requested during a performance crisis is often simply a knee-jerk reaction or a way of passing responsibility for the problem on to someone else.

An effective training intervention is one that analyses and considers all aspects of the situation, so resist being pressured into an immediate response or 'cure'. If the performance problem is an anticipated one, then how much lead-in time do you have? Does this allow you to phase the development over a period of time? When does the customer want the intervention to be completed? Is there a deadline or is it an open-ended process of development?

### The learner/s' likely entry behaviour

How much do the learners know about the current or anticipated performance problem? What is their likely reaction to it? Will they view it as a development opportunity or as a punishment for poor performance or failure? Much of this depends on the customer's attitude towards the learners. The organization's culture will also have a significant impact on the learners' perceptions of the proposed intervention. You will therefore need to negotiate with the customer on how the learners are to be briefed about any proposed intervention.

If you take the above factors into consideration when negotiating a design brief with a customer then the resulting training design has a much greater likelihood of being effective (see the Activity box).

## USING OCCUPATIONAL STANDARDS

There is one other factor that needs to be taken into consideration in the light of current changes in training and development: occupational standards.

## ACTIVITY

Using the factors we have identified for developing an effective design brief, identify the implications of not considering all the relevant factors? What could be the effects for the organization, for the individual, and for you?

Starting in the 1980s, a major revolution has been taking place in the world of training and development. Competence-based training and development, while not wholly replacing traditional vocational training and education, is becoming the norm in most vocational areas. This has wide-ranging implications for trainers and their customers. Whether carrying out a training needs analysis, negotiating a design brief, designing an intervention or assessing and evaluating the success of the intervention, occupational standards and outcome-based assessment emphasizing competence and capability are now a major influence.

Occupational standards directly address how someone performs in the workplace but they involve more than simply an observation of skill. The notion of competence includes the observable skill element of performance but it also includes the knowledge and understanding required to ensure effective performance. Below is an example of how this is affecting practising physicians and surgeons in Canada.

The Alberta College of Physicians and Surgeons is carrying out an evaluation every seven to ten years of practising physicians licensed by them. They are to be evaluated on their 'knowledge, skills and performance'. The college is considering methods of evaluating competence, such as examinations for measuring knowledge, surgery visits to assess skills, and patient surveys for gauging performance. The Federation of Medical Licensing Authorities in Canada is meeting in an attempt to standardize competence testing.

Occupational standards are therefore extremely important both for the trainer and for the customer and the learner. They allow you to identify the current competence of individuals or groups of people against a set of clearly identified standards for their particular occupational area. They allow you to negotiate outcomes in much more detail with the customer, and, in the UK along with some other countries, they provide learners with opportunities for obtaining National Vocational Qualifications. They can focus the design of the training intervention and can make the assessment of the learners and the evaluation of the effectiveness of the intervention much easier to quantify (see the Activity box).

## ACTIVITY

Identify any occupational standards available for the occupations for which you provide training and development interventions. At what levels are they available? If they are not available yet, when are they likely to be introduced?

## PRODUCING LEARNING OUTCOMES

The need to negotiate clearly identified outcomes when preparing a design brief was identified earlier in this chapter, and is vital to the eventual success of the training intervention. Failure to clearly identify expected outcomes can result in a poorly focused programme with no means of assessing its effectiveness.

The first stage is to identify the purpose of the training intervention. All those involved in the training intervention; trainers, managers, customers, learners, should share a common understanding of the purpose of the intervention. The purpose or aim of the intervention should be clearly visible within the design brief and should effectively focus the expectations of all those involved.

The aim is to produce a general statement of intent – what the intervention intends to achieve – and this is the link between the identified training need and the eventual design provision of the training intervention.

These statements are usually very broad, giving only a brief or superficial description of the intervention's intention, for example:

- to provide an induction for new employees;
- to develop managers' interviewing skills;
- to train new clerical staff in wordprocessing and desk-top publishing;
- to introduce customer care in all departments.

Their main function is to communicate clearly to all parties involved in the intervention an easily understood description of that intervention. They are of little operational use for the trainer who is designing the intervention, however, as they are vague statements and do not give sufficient detail about what the learner is expected to achieve. To do this we need clearly defined objectives.

### Performance objectives

Performance objectives clearly set out the standard of performance you intend learners to achieve at the end of the training intervention. When designing training therefore, the performance objectives are an important consideration. You may, however, experience a number of difficulties when attempting to identify performance objectives.

- The occupational standards may not yet be available.
- The training intervention may only be a starting point for the learner, for example, to develop their knowledge and understanding or raise their awareness about a particular issue.
- You may not be allowed sufficient time to be able to develop learners' competence to the appropriate level or standard.
- Facilities 'off-the-job' may not duplicate the working environment and therefore not match 'on-the-job' working conditions.
- If they are set at too high a level to be achieved within the context of the training intervention they can have a demotivating effect on the learner.

A direct consequence of these difficulties is the need to compromise, to develop more appropriate performance objectives for the particular training intervention. While for the majority of performance problems this is an acceptable compromise it is not possible in all situations.

In the majority of occupations the outcome of a training intervention is not a matter of life or death. If a typist doesn't format a letter properly then the result may only be embarrassing, if the machinist wrongly inserts a zip it will be picked up by quality control. However, for some occupational areas, and some aspects of others, the consequences of poor performance are much more serious.

For the emergency services, medical professions, pilots, building inspectors, health and safety personnel, first-aiders, to name but a few, poor performance can result in loss of life. For these groups of people trainers and their customers cannot afford to compromise on performance objectives. The learners must be competent before they are allowed to operate in their normal working environment, and must be competent to the standards laid down by their vocational or professional area, whether or not that area is yet competence-based.

So what do you do if there are not yet any occupational standards for your area of intervention, or if they are not appropriate for the design brief you have negotiated with your customer? You write your own!

## Writing performance objectives

Performance objectives contain three essential components (see Figure 4.3):

1. A statement of the performance to be demonstrated by the learner.
2. A statement of the range of conditions under which the learner needs to be able to demonstrate that performance.
3. A statement of the minimum acceptable standards of performance the learner must demonstrate.

The three components are essential to enable you to identify the theoretical and practical content of the training intervention, to ensure that it contains sufficient relevance to normal or expected working conditions that maximum transfer of learning can take place and to

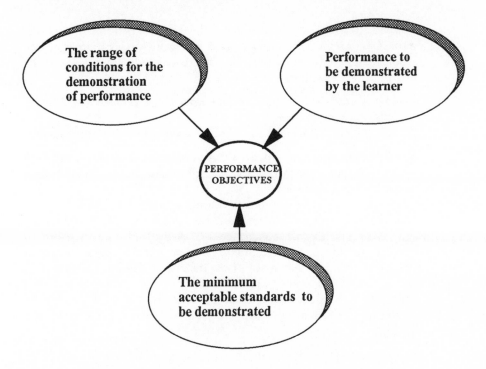

**Figure 4.3** *Performance objectives*

enable accurate assessment of the learner's progress against the objectives.

Remember, the performance objectives are clear statements of what the learner will be able to do as a result of the training intervention. Not only do they help you design the intervention but they also clearly communicate to the learner what is expected of them (see the Activity box).

## ACTIVITY

How can the three essential components of performance objectives help the trainer, the learner and the customer?

When designing a training intervention or learning event there is a further reason for ensuring that the performance objectives you identify are clear and unambiguous. This is because it may not always be you who are going to be delivering that particular event or intervention. It is your responsibility therefore to ensure that they are written in such a way as to clearly indicate the required outcomes in order that outcomes are standardized.

The objective should be clearly stated in terms of performance and the verbs used in the performance statements should clearly indicate the actions required of the learner. This difference can be clearly seen in the following two examples.

1. The learner will be able to understand the principles of cardio-pulmonary resuscitation.
2. The learner will be able to perform cardio-pulmonary resuscitation.

The first example is too woolly. What does understand mean? How do we know it will work in practice? Therefore how do we know to what extent knowing about it is useful?

The second example is much clearer. It states what the learner is expected to be able to *do*. It indicates the *actions* required by the learner and leaves little room for interpretation. Active verbs are therefore an essential component of a performance objective. If it does not contain an active verb then it is not an acceptable statement. Without any indication of the actions the learner will be required to demonstrate it is almost impossible to measure success with any certainty.

You need to avoid objectives written in non-performance terms. For example:

- will know how to measure blood pressure;
- will be able to understand the need for record-keeping;
- will believe the need for non-discrimination;
- will perceive the difference between safe and unsafe passenger transportation.

## ACTIVITY

Using either a training intervention you are already involved in that does not have clearly identified performance objectives, or a training intervention you are in the process of designing, write appropriate performance objectives.

## SUMMARY

This chapter has focused on the underpinning knowledge of learning and its design which is required to ensure your competence, and therefore your effectiveness, as a trainer in a wide range of roles and situations.

It began by exploring the role that learning plays within a training intervention. The four major ways that learning can take place were identified and you were encouraged to explore your current training practice in terms of which combinations of the four methods were used in your training interventions.

The learning cycle was identified and discussed and its relevance to the training and development process was explored. Links were also made between the learning cycle and the way people prefer to learn. As a result of this the factors to be considered when designing a learning event were considered and a strategy for developing a design brief outlined. The importance of involving the customer was stressed and emphasis placed on the role of negotiation when designing a training brief.

Occupational standards of competence, as well as other forms of outcome-based qualifications and their impact on training and development were explored and the relationship between standards and performance identified. You were then able to explore the process of developing learning outcomes, including their relationship with occupational standards and the identified performance problem.

## References

Honey, P and Mumford, A (1986) *Using Your Learning Styles*, second edition, Peter Honey, Ardingley House, 10 Linden Avenue, Maidenhead.

Honey, P and Mumford, A (1992) *Manual of Learning Styles*, third edition, Honey, Maidenhead.

Kolb, D A, Rubin, I M and McIntyre, J M (1974) *Organizational Psychology: An Experiential Approach*, Prentice Hall, New Jersey.

Manpower Services Commission (1981) *Glossary of Training Terms*, MSC, HMSO, London.

## Further useful reading

Anderson, A H (1993) *Successful Training Practice*, Blackwell, Oxford. (Chapter 3 is very useful if you want to find our more about learning theories.)

Buckley, R and Caple, J (1994) *The Theory and Practice of Training*, third edition, Kogan Page, London.

Clark, N (1992) *Managing Personal Learning and Change: A Trainer's Guide*, McGraw Hill, London.

Cotton, J (1995) *The Theory of Learning*, Kogan Page, London.

Harrison, R (1992) *Employee Development*, IPM, London. (Chapter 7 looks in more detail at different theories of learning and puts them in the context of the learning organization.)

Mager, R (1991) *Developing Attitudes Towards Learning*, second edition, Kogan Page, London.

Reid, M A, Barrington, H and Kenney, J (1992) *Training Interventions*, third edition, IPM, London. (Chapter 3 discusses in some detail the links between learning and training and explores theories of learning in some depth.)

Sheal, P (1994) *How to Develop and Present Staff Training Courses*, second edition, Kogan Page, London.

## 5

## Delivering and developing

## INTRODUCTION

Once you have written clear and accurate performance objectives you will be in a position to identify the most effective or appropriate type of intervention to support the development of the learner/s. This chapter focuses on the key issues of training design and delivery. It begins by identifying types of training intervention before moving on to look at the influence entry behaviour may have on the learners and the intervention.

Once these factors have been considered then it becomes possible to design or adapt resources specific to that intervention and its performance outcomes. The final factor in the equation of effective training design and delivery is that of learning transfer.

## TYPES OF TRAINING INTERVENTION

There are a range of interventions available to choose from. However, the type or types you select will depend on a number of factors (see Figure 5.1):

- The number of learners.
- The aims and objectives of the intervention.
- The resources available.
- The timescale.
- The amount of support available within the organization.
- Production/organization demands.

At this stage we are trying to identify the most appropriate form that the intervention could take. In other words, we are developing an intervention strategy, and, in broad terms, it will either be on-the-job, off-the-job or a combination of both.

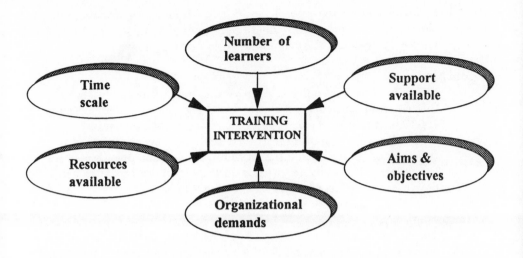

**Figure 5.1** *Factors influencing choice of training intervention*

## On-the-job training

As this suggests, the intervention takes place wholly within the learner's actual working environment. This used to be known as the 'sitting next to Nelly' strategy. Historically the majority of training at skill level took place in this way. New operatives were sat next to a skilled operative (Nelly) and learned their job by observation and imitation. Training in this manner was often unstructured and simply occurred on an *ad hoc* basis. There were no clearly identified aims and objectives (other than to get the new operative up to production standard as quickly as possible). 'Nelly' was also operating under normal working or production pressures and therefore couldn't focus all her (or his) attention on the trainee's progress.

Not only was it unplanned, unstructured and poorly monitored but also bad habits were passed on along with the good working practices. There were advantages to this strategy, however. The skill was learned under normal operating conditions. This meant that the tools or other equipment were the same as the learner was expected to use during their work. The learning was seen as relevant by the learner as it was within their eventual working environment. It was therefore intensely practical. It also appeared less costly to employers who did not have to bear the direct expense of a number of trainers.

On-the-job training can be more effectively structured than this, however. Also, if the training intervention is taking place in the context of occupational standards, then it is necessary to be able to assess performance on-the-job. There are a number of training and development methods you could select from that are appropriate for on-the-job training. They are discussed in outline below.

## Coaching

This method is derived from a conscious recognition that people are able to learn from everything they do. Coaching, by a manager or more experienced colleagues, can support the learner's development by helping them solve a problem or to carry out a task more effectively than before. It is focused on developing the individual to meet the objectives of the job. While it is possible to coach a small group of learners at the same time it is most effective when used for one-to-one learning.

## Mentoring

This is more commonly used when developing managers as, unlike coaching, it concentrates on developing the skills required to carry out a particular role rather than a particular task. It is akin to 'taking someone under your wing' in that the personal development of the individual learner is very much the objective of this method.

## Learning contracts

This is a three-way or tripartite process. A contract is agreed between the learner, a member of the learner's organization (preferably their line-manager or supervisor) and the learner's tutor or training and development adviser (TDA). The contract determines precisely what learning needs to be done, how it is to be done, by when, the resources required to facilitate its success and what evidence is required to show that the learning outcomes have been achieved. It is an extremely flexible method of development and can be used both for personal development and for the development of practical skills.

## Secondment and job rotation

This used to be used almost exclusively for management development purposes, but, with increasing flexibility in many organizations as well as their de-layering, ie taking out levels of management, it is now used at a number of levels in an organization. It has developed from the belief that exposure to different people, different jobs, different approaches and different contexts will broaden the employee's view of their organization and their role within it, while at the same time providing a wide range of learning opportunities. This is more usually a long-term intervention although short-term secondments, up to three months, are occasionally used. Secondment may be to another organization, although more usually the employee is seconded to a different department within their organization. If this is only a short-term move it is more usual to refer to it as job-rotation.

This is a useful strategy when developing multi-skilled operatives in either production or service environments. To simply move people around the organization in an *ad hoc* way however is not an effective training and development intervention. It needs to be carefully planned and monitored to ensure that the learning objectives identified at the beginning of the process are being realized. This method could be used in conjunction with the learning contract strategy identified earlier.

## Job instruction

This is the 'new, improved and updated version' of sitting next to Nelly. It is systematic and uses the following stages:

1. Tell the learner how to do the job.
2. Show the learner how to do the job.
3. Allow the learner to do the job under supervision.

It is eminently suitable for skill development as the job is broken down into stages. The stages are then practised until the learner is able to consistently demonstrate the skill.

All the above methods have at least one thing in common – they rely on the structured and informed support of the learner's organization. This could be in terms of resources, time, or – equally important – skilled TDAs, managers and supervisors. It is not therefore a 'cheap' option for the organization. On-the-job training is not simply 'sitting next to Nelly'. It needs to be planned, structured and resourced as carefully as off-the-job training.

If your organization currently does not use on-the-job training, try to identify why this is so. Could it be incorporated into any future design strategies by using any of the methods identified above? Would it enhance the learning opportunities available to the learner?

## Off-the-job training

As this suggests, the intervention takes place away from the learner's usual working environment. Historically this has been seen as 'the training course option'. A manager identifies, correctly or otherwise, a performance problem and contacts the training department to tell them he wants a training course run for these people. Indeed, many training departments still only operate on the basis of a menu of training courses run throughout the year. Imagine the scenario described below.

The training department sends out the menu of courses to managers and supervisors and asks for nominations. The supervisors and managers use some method for selecting individuals (which often has nothing to do with whether they 'need' the training), the individuals are told they are going on the course and then hear no more until they turn up at the training centre one Monday morning.

Unfortunately this scenario is very common, even in the so-called enlightened organizations. Off-the-job training interventions need to be well structured and to relate directly to the usual or potential working environment of the learner. Also, if the training intervention is taking place in the context of occupational standards then off-the-job training will normally only form part of any intervention. A number of potential methods are outlined below.

### Training course

This is the traditional 'off-the-job' method.

- It could take place on the employer's premises, at a college or university, with a specialist training provider or consultant, etc.
- It could be an internal course or an external course.
- It could consist of learners all from the same organization or could have a mix of learners from other organizations.
- It could last anything from a half-day upwards.
- It could take place on a day release basis over a number of months or years or could be in a block of days or weeks.
- It needs to be clearly structured and to have well-defined learning outcomes.

### Distance, open and flexible learning

While there are a number of practical differences between distance, open and flexible learning, their aims are the same. Essentially, learners are provided with a series of materials that they are required to work through with the support of a telephone tutor and sometimes workshops. Various tasks are completed and assessed and sometimes there is a formal examination at the end of the programme of work. It requires learners to be very disciplined in their approach to the work as the onus is upon the individual to meet deadlines. The selection of learners and the quality of the materials are two of the most important considerations if choosing this method of intervention.

### Workshops

Workshops are generally very participative events which bring together a number of individual learners who want to develop in a particular skill area. They are particularly useful for developing 'people' skills such as assertiveness, negotiation, managing meetings, etc, but are also useful for developing knowledge and understanding of more complex issues. They allow newly developing interpersonal skills to be practised in a sheltered and supportive environment and also provide the opportunity for giving and receiving feedback.

### Outdoor development

This is often used as a management development method and usually focuses on the development of team-building and leadership skills. It can also be used to develop communication, planning, problem-solving and other people management and resource management skills. It is usually of the 'short, sharp shock' style where individuals are required to rely on the resources of the group and where failure produces immediate feedback.

Properly structured and facilitated it can provide an extremely powerful learning environment.

## Computer-based training

This is usually in the form of a Learning Unit. A commonly seen example of this is the computerized typing tutor. A computer programme provides a structured learning opportunity for the individual learner to develop at their own pace. It provides feedback through knowledge of results and offers suggestions for progression. There is also software available that can develop and assess learners' knowledge and understanding of a particular area. The technology is still relatively costly and programmes can only be written and adapted by experts. It also requires the learner to have a relatively high level of motivation.

## Self-development

Again, this is a method most commonly used for developing managers. It requires the learner to take responsibility for their own development. Unfortunately, in many organizations it means exactly that – get on with it! It is seized upon as a way of making economies on the training and development budget. Effective self-development can be enhanced by an appraisal system. Goals are identified and negotiated and, where appropriate, organization resources are made available to support the learner.

Obviously this is not an exhaustive account of all available training and development strategies but simply a brief introduction to those most commonly used. Most training interventions will be developed using a combination of on-the-job and off-the-job methods. It is unlikely that a perfect match will be found between the most effective intervention and the solution of the performance problem but by taking the above factors into consideration an acceptable and workable compromise can be achieved.

## ACTIVITY

What strategies do you currently use in the training interventions you are involved in? What are their advantages and disadvantages when related to the identified performance problem? Could another strategy be more effective?

## THE INFLUENCE OF ENTRY BEHAVIOUR

The design of every training intervention should be based on the difference between the performance objectives identified in the design brief and the learner's entry behaviour. This is the competence gap – the difference between the skills, knowledge and understanding required by the learner to perform effectively or competently and the skills, knowledge and understanding currently held by the learner.

The learner is so often the unknown ingredient in our recipe to 'cure' a performance problem. We can set out the aims and objectives of the intervention in clear and unambiguous terms. We can develop and agree a strategy for the overall delivery of the intervention. But what about the learners? In some situations we may be fortunate enough to have a clearly defined group of learners who have similar performance levels and similar abilities. Increasingly more realistic is the scenario where interventions are being designed to cope with a rapidly changing work environment; and also where learners are expected to take on some different responsibilities in addition to a role they already have experience in.

This often means we are involved in developing more mature and experienced learners, sometimes where traditional knowledge and skills have become redundant and where there might be quite high anxiety levels about either their job-security or the demands of a new role. This can make them quite reluctant learners. What we describe as entry behaviour includes:

- The existing skill, knowledge and understanding held by the learner.
- The attitudes held by the learner.
- The expectations held by the learner.

As Figure 5.2 shows, these are interactive.

The following questions may help you to begin planning for the entry behaviour of learners.

1. How many learners are there?
2. Do you know what the learners' current competence is?
3. Do you know the extent of their development needs?
4. Are the learners the symptom or the cause of the performance problem?
5. Are the learners involved willingly or are they reluctant learners?
6. Are there likely to be major differences in current competence between learners?
7. Are there likely to be major differences in learning ability between learners?

The answers to these questions will begin to give you a broad picture of the learners' anticipated entry behaviour. If there is more than one learner the picture becomes less clear. When faced with a group of learners problems of unpredictable learning behaviour become magnified (see the Activity box).

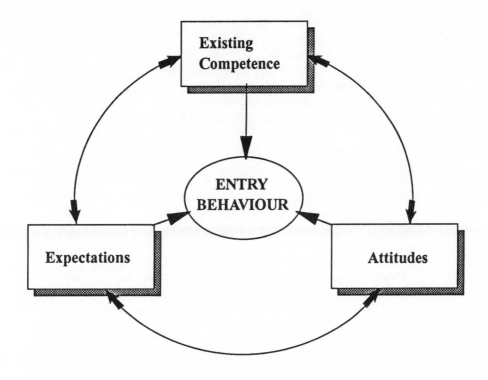

**Figure 5.2** *Influences on entry behaviour*

**ACTIVITY**

How do you currently identify learners' entry behaviour?

In response to the Activity exercise, you could identify learners' entry behaviour by:

● interviewing learners, line managers and other trainers;
● using questionnaires;
● testing learners before the intervention;
● examining existing records.

Identifying entry behaviour will assist in the design of the intervention by helping to determine the starting point in terms of skills, knowledge and understanding. It can also assist in estimating the time required to enable the learner to achieve competent performance. If learners are assessed in some way before the intervention, for example, through the administering of specific tests or by observing performance, any remedial needs the learner has to bring them up to the level of other learners can be identified and addressed.

Providing an effective learning environment requires us to consider learners' motivation, to reduce anxiety, to ensure there are adequate and relevant learning opportunities to participate, practise and perform competently and to provide performance feedback. Also, when we are planning for a group of learners we have to try to achieve a 'best-fit' between the aims and objectives of the intervention and the needs and abilities of the learners.

If you work for an external training provider or are a consultant to the organization, you may not meet the learners until they walk through the door of the training room. The less we know or are able to find out about our prospective learners the more assumptions we are required to make and the more assumptions we make the more we risk the training intervention failing to match the competence gap.

Once we have determined, as far as possible, the learners' entry behaviour, we can then use this information to plan the training intervention in much more detail. So far we have the design brief and an overall strategy encompassing one or more of the methods identified earlier. Now that we have information on learners' entry behaviour we can begin to select delivery methods and the most appropriate level at which to begin the delivery of the intervention (see the Activity box).

## ACTIVITY

Using the next training intervention you are required to design as the basis for this activity, indicate how you are identifying the entry behaviour of the learners. How are you accommodating this in your design?

## DEVELOPING AND ADAPTING RESOURCES

Another aspect of your role in the design of a training intervention is the development of resources to support the learner. This could mean designing new materials from scratch or, if more appropriate, the adaptation of existing materials. In this chapter we are only discussing the development of training resources such as handouts, OHP slides, case studies, etc. The identification and allocation of other physical and material resources such as rooms, equipment and personnel will be addressed in chapter 7 (p. 125).

These resources are not simply confined to the delivery of the intervention, however. It is also necessary to look at the development of resources to identify current levels of competence in learners, either individuals or groups, as well as resources to assess the development of the learning during and at the end of the intervention.

We are going to focus therefore on the following:

1. Developing or adapting training and development materials.
2. Developing or adapting visual aids and support materials.
3. Developing or adapting self-assessment materials for learners.
4. Developing or adapting tests to assess knowledge and understanding.
5. Developing or adapting support mechanisms for learners.

This should cover most of the eventualities you will be confronted with when designing and developing a training intervention.

## Developing or adapting training and development materials

These materials can take a number of forms. It could be a handout to demonstrate some principles of knowledge, a case study, a group or individual exercise. It could be a workbook or handbook or an open learning unit. But whatever format the materials take they will have a number of things in common. They need to be clearly written and clearly laid out – the same rules that apply to report writing also apply here.

1. Make sure there is a title or heading that clearly states the purpose of the document.
2. If it is a long document, use headings and sub-headings to break up the text.
3. Use short sentences and short paragraphs and leave plenty of 'white space'.
4. Use lists of bullet points to summarize information rather than using long, dense paragraphs.
5. Check-lists can be very useful and practical documents for learners.
6. If you use tables or diagrams make sure they are clearly labelled.
7. If there is a lot of text use double line spacing to make the document seem less dense.
8. Make sure it is professionally presented, a photocopy of a photocopy of a photocopy just looks messy.

The materials need to be directly relevant to the learning outcomes. This is particularly important when using a standard set of materials. It may be necessary to adapt materials, either in whole or in part, to put them into an appropriate context for the learner. Not only will relevant materials enhance the transfer of learning back to the workplace but it will also help to maintain the motivation of the learner by placing new material within the context of the learner's existing knowledge and experience.

Developing resources from scratch can be a very expensive process, particularly at the level of workbook or open learning unit. Even writing a simple case study takes time to research if it is to be relevant to the learner. It is usually for reasons of cost that the decision is made to use or adapt existing resources. Be prepared to be ruthless with existing materials, either in their use or adaptation. Materials can quickly become dated and irrelevant. Remember, the purpose of training materials is to support the development of the learner, if it is not directly relevant to the learner's achieving the identified learning objectives – don't use it!

---

**Important note**
When modifying or adapting existing materials be aware of any copyright restrictions that apply. If you are adapting something that you or a colleague previously developed then this is not likely to be a problem. Otherwise, check with the copyright holders that what you are proposing to do is legally permissible.

---

### ACTIVITY

Analyse the materials you currently use in your training interventions. Do they meet the criteria outlined here? How could you improve them?

## Developing or adapting visual aids and support materials

The use of visual aids can greatly enhance the amount of information retained by the learner. Many learning events consist of the verbal presentation of information, sometimes coupled with practical experience of the topic being discussed. Research has demonstrated that only about 25–30 per cent of information presented in this way is retained by the learner. Using visual images to support and reinforce the spoken word can double the amount of information retained.

Effective visual aids can therefore greatly enhance the communication between the learner and the trainer and can therefore also speed the attainment of learning objectives, and, hence, competence. They have many benefits both for the learner and the trainer when designed and used competently. However, I have sat through many training presentations where the design and use of the visual aids used by the trainer was embarrassing, if not for the trainer, then certainly for the audience of learners.

Visual aids include overhead projector slides, flipcharts, black/whiteboards, slides, photographs and videos. Their benefits can be seen in Figure 5.3. By following a few simple rules you can design and use them effectively.

1. Fit the medium to the audience and the topic. Simple is best. A good presentation can be ruined by overkill.

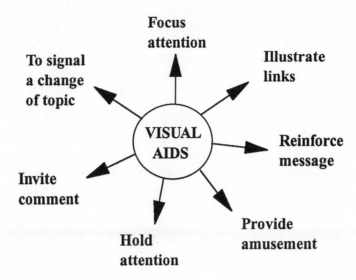

**Figure 5.3** *Benefits of visual aids*

2. Plan the presentation, whether it is a formal lecture or an element of an informal workshop.
3. Once you have identified your objectives decide where they can be enhanced by visual aids.
4. Prepare your choice of visual aids following the guidelines suggested below.
5. Rehearse the presentation and check any equipment prior to its use.
6. Clearly inform the learners when introducing the aid as to its purpose and relevance.

## Overhead projector slide

This is a very flexible method of visual reinforcement. It can be used to deliver anything from a simple hand-written message to a complex multi-coloured and multi-layered image. You can show the whole image or only part by masking with paper. Photocopying on to acetate can also produce clear images of quite complex diagrams or desk-top-published material. These guidelines should help.

1. Make sure that the projector is set up in such a position that the image can be seen by all of the audience. Too many OHP slides are spoiled by the top of the OHP getting in the way.
2. Make sure that the lens and projection glass is clean. This will ensure quality of projection.
3. Keep the transparency simple: aim for only one topic per sheet.
4. Aim for no more than 4–6 words on a line and no more than 6–8 lines if you are presenting written information. Any more than this and the print size becomes too small to read comfortably.
5. Use it to emphasize only the major points of your verbal presentation, not as a word-for-word account of what you are saying.

6. Remove the transparency as soon as you have made your point and, if required, the audience has made a note of its contents. It can be much more effective, however, if you make paper copies of any transparencies you wish the audience to make note of. This enables the learner to concentrate on what you are saying rather than hurriedly trying to write everything down before you remove it.

7. Switch off the machine before removing the transparency and switch it back on when you have placed the next transparency on to the glass. This avoids distraction by a bright, white screen.

8. Remember to talk to the audience and not to the screen. If you need to read from the transparency, position yourself so that you can read from it on the glass. Too many presenters make the mistake of turning their back on the audience to read from the screen.

9. If you wish to point to something on the transparency, point to it on the glass using a pen or special pointer. Don't turn your back on the audience to point to it on the screen.

If you follow these simple steps your OHP visual aids will effectively enhance your spoken message.

## Flipcharts

Flipcharts have many advantages as visual aids. They are easily portable, they can be prepared fully in advance, they can be used for brainstorming and other group activities and their contents can be displayed around the room (with a little help from Blu-tack!). They are also dynamic, in that you can add to the drawing or main points during your discussion with the group.

1. Instead of relying on drawing free-hand, pencil in the lines before the presentation. This will make the end product appear much more professional.

2. You can also pencil in 'memory joggers' on one of the corners of the flipchart paper. The audience won't be able to see them but you will be able to check that you have covered the main points.

3. Make sure that what you write or draw can be seen by the learners. Use thick lines and deep colours and make sure your writing is big enough and clear enough. If you feel that you can't rely on the quality of your writing, pencil it in beforehand.

4. Most of us view flipcharts as a spur-of-the-moment visual aid but it needs as much planning as the use of transparencies if it is to be effective.

5. As with OHP transparencies, remember to face the audience if you are talking to them. Stand to the side of the flipchart and try to face the audience as you write. if you can't manage this, don't talk and write at the same time.

6. If you are using a flipchart that you have already prepared try to ensure that there is a blank sheet between each visual. this has the same effect as switching off the OHP. It indicates to the learner a change in focus.

<table>
<tr><td>

## ACTIVITY

Review the visual aids you use in your training interventions. Do they follow the guidelines identified here? How can you improve them?

</td></tr>
</table>

## Developing or adapting self-assessment materials for learners

So far we have concentrated on developing materials relevant to the development of skill, knowledge and understanding. As trainers however, we are also involved in encouraging the learner to take responsibility for their own development. We can begin this process by encouraging them to identify the skills, knowledge and understanding they already have. We can also encourage learners to assess their development during and after the training intervention. One of the most effective, and simplest, methods is to use a self-assessment grid. In the UK a number of these have been produced by NVQ Communications and are called Skillscan. For example, there are Skillscans for all levels of NVQ in training and development. They ask you to compare the performance outcomes to what you already do at work and you have to rate the frequency that you carry out these activities from often, sometimes or never. If you do not have access to ready-published self-assessment documents you can construct your own using the same principles.

Alternatively, or to complement the self-assessment grid, you may choose to use self-administered tests to enable learners to assess the development of their knowledge and understanding. In order to help them assess their current competence you will also need to make available to them relevant performance information. This includes current expectations of competence, anticipated competence requirements, any appropriate occupational standards, and the learning objectives of the intervention.

Without this information the learner will be unable to effectively identify current competence. Unfortunately, the identification of current competence is often confined to a pre-course questionnaire. This would be acceptable if the questionnaire contained the information outlined above. In most instances, however, it simply consists of a number of general questions such as:

1. What does your current role consist of?
2. What three things would you like to get from this course?
3. What are your strengths and weaknesses?
4. What are your objectives for this course?

The problem with these types of questions however is they do not really tell us anything of value about the learner, and the learner usually views it as a chore to complete. If we seriously wish to involve the learner in the process of self-assessment, then we need to ensure that what we ask them to do has relevance for them and is something they can take ownership of.

---

## ACTIVITY

What self-assessment methods do you currently use with learners? How can you improve them?

---

## Developing or adapting tests to assess knowledge and understanding

For some occupational areas there will already be some standardized tests available. They are often produced commercially, usually by an examining body. They will have been designed by specialists in both testing and the occupational area and should have been subjected to rigorous testing to assess their validity and reliability.

Such tests may not be appropriate for all your training and development interventions, however. You may only be developing a small part of the knowledge and understanding requirements for a particular occupational area, or, the knowledge and understanding you wish to develop and assess may not have standardized tests available. In these instances you will need to develop specific tests that are customized to the needs of your organization or that of your customers.

There are two main methods you can use to assess the knowledge and understanding of your learners:

1. Objective testing.
2. Subjective testing.

There are a number of differences between objective and subjective tests. Primarily, objective tests usually have only one correct answer which has been predetermined by the trainer, whereas subjective tests use questions that are much more open-ended, for example, 'How would you negotiate .........?' Also, objective tests are most often used when assessing specific, technical information whereas subjective tests can elicit information concerning performance, knowledge and understanding. What all methods have in common, however, is that they should relate only to the specific knowledge and understanding requirements of the learning objectives.

### Objective testing

This is the most common method used to test the knowledge and understanding of the learner. It can be administered verbally or as a written test. If it is pre-planned and issued to all learners then it is referred to as a pre-set questionnaire. It is possible to assess all aspects of knowledge acquisition. These include:

1. Factual analysis.
2. Factual recall.
3. Comprehension, ie, understanding.
4. Application of facts.

A questionnaire can test one or more of these aspects. There are a number of different ways you can test knowledge and understanding objectively and they are described briefly below.

**Multiple choice**   The learner is asked a question or given a statement and has to choose an answer from a list of possible responses, usually a choice of four or five.

**Multiple response**   This is very similar to multiple choice but there may be more than one correct response.

**True/false and yes/no questions**   The learner has to decide whether the statement is true or false or whether the answer to the question is yes or no.

**Matching items**   The learner is given two lists and has to match items from list A to items in list B.

**Sequencing**   The learner is given a jumbled list of objects or processes and has to place the items in the correct order or sequence.

**Completion exercises**   The learner has to complete a statement or a list of information from memory.

**Factual recall**   The learner is asked for a specific piece of information.

One of the most useful factors of objective testing is that the learners can assess themselves. While in some situations it may be necessary for the trainer to administer the test, if the test is being used for developmental purposes, ie, to assess how far the learners have progressed so far, then the learners should be able to request the test and complete it themselves.

As an objective test has standardized answers, then learners can assess their own performance against the answer grid. As long as the trainer is available at some stage to provide feedback on this performance the learner can take responsibility for the assessment of their knowledge and understanding. This is not possible with more subjective forms of assessment.

## Subjective testing

This includes setting assignments, writing reports and essays and responding to case studies. This type of testing is attempting to assess the development of the learner's ability to organize, analyse, interpret and express more complex concepts, processes or ideas. It is much more difficult for the trainer to evaluate and assess the learner's development using these methods as there is no 'right' answer to most of these problems.

Subjective testing can also use questioning and interviews to provide immediate feedback from the learner in terms of their current level of knowledge and understanding. It is also invaluable when assessing learners with some special needs, eg, literacy problems or visual impairment, where the aim is to test the learner's level of knowledge and understanding rather than their reading or writing ability.

## ACTIVITY

Provide examples of both objective and subjective tests YOU have designed to assess the knowledge and understanding of learners.

### Developing or adapting support mechanisms for learners

Developing resources to support the development and assessment of the learner is only part of the process, however. You also need to ensure that there are systems in place to support the learner using the materials you have developed. Whatever resources you have developed, it is unlikely that they can be used in isolation. Learners need support, advice and feedback but it is not always essential that it comes from you. Bringing together a group of learners all going through the same process can provide a resource that you, the trainer, can use.

Sharing experiences, assessing each other's performance, offering advice and feedback can be just as valid from another learner as it can be from the trainer.

## ACTIVITY

What learner support systems do you currently use?

## TRANSFERRING LEARNING

The final area we need to address when exploring the design and delivery of learning is ensuring that the learning that takes place can be transferred to the normal working environment. It is only when this takes place that the training intervention can be said to be effective. Broad and Newstrom (1992) define it as:

*... the effective and continuing application, by trainees to their jobs, of the knowledge and skills gained in training – both on and off the job.*

Some aspects of learning transfer have already been referred to in this chapter, for example, the use of different equipment from that used in the normal working environment, or, the lack of normal production pressures on the learner. Also, we often have the expectation that the learner can apply and transfer previous learning. This is only a valid expectation if the learners themselves are able to identify similarities between what they are expected to do now and what they have previously learned.

This application of learning to work, or learning transfer as it is more commonly known, is obviously accomplished much more easily if the training takes place on-the-job. But, as we have seen earlier, this is not always practical or desirable. By creating a safe working environment for training away from normal working conditions we can inhibit the transfer of learning. If the learning is not consolidated back in the workplace through practice of the newly learned skills or use of the newly acquired knowledge, then the learner is more likely to forget what has been learned as a result of the intervention.

It is therefore essential to enlist the support of the learner's supervisor or line manager and, where appropriate, the learner's peers. This is often avoided as it is seen as the trainer's responsibility to develop the learner, but for newly acquired learning to be consolidated the learner needs to have opportunities to practise. If their role does not allow them to use their newly acquired skills then you need to ask why they were trained in the first instance. There are a number of methods you can use to facilitate the transfer of learning to the workplace, while at the same time increasing the involvement of line managers and supervisors in the process.

● Action plans.
● Learning contracts.
● Individual projects.
● Follow-up through guidance and coaching.
● Training or personal development plans.
● Review workshops.

## Action plans

An action plan helps the learner to look at the way they do their job now and then identify how they can improve what they do by applying their newly acquired skills. It is a plan to put training into practice in the workplace. It should identify what is to be achieved, by when, what support is required to enable the transfer to take place, and some means of reviewing progress. Ideally the learner's line manager or supervisor should also be involved.

## Learning contracts

Earlier in this chapter these were referred to as a development method, but they can also be used to consolidate learning that has taken place off-the-job.

## Individual projects

An individual project tailored to the learner's job role can greatly enhance the transfer of newly acquired skills and knowledge to the workplace. For example, a supervisor who has recently completed a marketing programme could be given a project that includes an immediate analysis of the organization's marketing strategy along with detailed recommendations for its further development. This allows the learner to review, consolidate, reinforce and apply the skills and knowledge learned during the training intervention.

## Follow-up through guidance and coaching

This was also identified as a development method earlier in the chapter. It has great potential as a consolidation strategy but will only be effective if the line manager or supervisor involved is skilled in guidance and coaching. Unfortunately, in many organizations this is not the case and learners and supervisors are just told to 'get on with it!'.

## Training or personal development plans

Some larger organizations use Continuous Development Plans to assist in the training and development of the workforce. These operate by identifying the key skills required for each role and include transferable or generic skills. Regular review of the learner's performance takes place, and plans to consolidate learning are incorporated.

A personal training and development plan is another means by which progress can be monitored. The plan is drawn up before the training intervention, usually as a result of the training needs analysis. The aims and objectives of the intervention are then clearly related to the needs of the learner. The learner can then plan, along with their supervisor, the best means of implementing the newly acquired knowledge and skill on return to the workplace.

## Review workshop

This is a useful follow-up to a training intervention, particularly one that was skill-based. Learners bring along their action plans and discuss progress to date. Any difficulties they have encountered are thrown open to the group and possible solutions are discussed.

This has just been a brief overview of the strategies and methods you can adopt to aid the transfer of learning from the training intervention to the workplace. Some will be more appropriate for your learners and their organization than others. What is important is that learning transfer takes place; leaving it to chance is a very risky business.

## ACTIVITY

How do you currently ensure that learning transfer takes place as a result of the training interventions you are involved in? How can you improve the rate of transfer?

## SUMMARY

After identifying the factors likely to affect your choice of training and development strategies you were introduced to a range of potential training interventions. You were then in a position to begin to negotiate the development strategy most likely to support the achievement of the intervention's outcomes. Once this was established the next step was to address the influence the entry behaviour of the learner/s was likely to have on any planned intervention. Methods for obtaining information from and about learners were identified and suggestions given about the best use of this information.

You were then encouraged to examine the development of resources to support the development and assessment of the learner. The importance of relevance was stressed and means of supporting self-assessment by the learners discussed. Finally, the need to transfer learning to the workplace was established along with strategies to facilitate this.

## References

Broad, M L and Newstrom, J W (1992) *Transfer of Training*, Addison Wesley, Massachusetts.

NVQ Communications (1993) *Skillscan: Training and Development, Level 4*, HMSO, London.

## Further useful reading

Anderson, A H (1993) *Successful Training Practice*, Blackwell, Oxford. (Chapter 5 is a comprehensive guide to design and development and includes an exploration of the impact of the motivation of the learner.)

Buckley, R and Caple, J (1991) *One-to-one Training and Coaching Skills*, Kogan Page, London.

Buckley, R and Caple, J (1994) *The Theory and Practice of Training*, third edition, Kogan Page, London.

Clements, P and Spinks, T (1993) *A Practical Guide to Facilitation Skills*, Kogan Page, London.

Davis, J (1992) *How to Write a Training Manual*, Gower, Aldershot.

Flegg, D and McHale, J (1991) *Selecting Training Aids*, Kogan Page, London. (This will give the less experienced trainer a good grounding in the effective selection of resources to support a training intervention.)

Fletcher, S (1991) *Designing Competence-based Training*, Kogan Page, London.

Hart, L B (1992) *Training Methods that Work*, Kogan Page, London.

Leigh, D (1991) *A Practical Approach to Group Training*, Kogan Page, London.

Mager, R (1991) *Making Instruction Work*, Kogan Page, London.

Nicolay, C and Barrette, J (1992) *Assembling Course Materials*, Kogan Page, London.

Parsloe, E (1992) *Coaching, Mentoring and Assessing. A practical guide to developing competence*, Kogan Page, London.

Powers, B (1992) *Instructor Excellence*, Jossey-Bass Publishers, San Francisco. (Part 2, chapters 5–10 cover: supplementary reading on being prepared, generating participation, course content and sequencing, dealing with questions and enhancing learning.)

Sheal, P (1994) *How to Develop and Present Staff Training Courses*, second edition, Kogan Page, London.

Stimson, N (1991) *How to Write and Prepare Training Materials*, Kogan Page, London. (This is a useful guide to the preparation of training materials whether you are a novice or experienced trainer.)

# 6

## Identifying the need

### INTRODUCTION

As trainers we are found more often than not at the delivery end of training. We design and deliver training programmes, courses, packages etc. Sometimes we even get to evaluate the effectiveness of what we have designed and delivered but, in most cases, we have not been involved in identifying the performance problem that led to the training intervention. As a result of this we are often expected to perform miracles and a number of issues often combine to support this view. This chapter focuses on those issues and the factors that contribute to them. It indicates strategies (tools) you can use to identify performance problems against different levels of requirement such as organization, individual, job and task, and will begin to equip you with the knowledge you need to undertake such analyses.

### GETTING INVOLVED

It does not matter if you are the only trainer in your organization or a member of a large training unit, you share many things in common:

- you want to perform effectively;
- you want recognition for your contribution to the success of the organization;
- you want to at least maintain the current quality of your contribution, and, where possible, enhance it;
- you want your learners to be committed to their own development;
- you want to keep your job!

All these factors are related to the way training is perceived in your organization and this perception can have an effect at all levels. If the recipients of the intervention are unhappy with what they are getting then this is generally communicated to their supervisors or managers. This can then affect their perception of the training and development function and they can reinforce the negative perceptions held by their subordinates. This can end up in a vicious circle where neither party can 'see the point' of all of this training business.

This directly affects you and your colleagues and the training function generally within the organization. It can place the training function under serious threat, particularly where the culture of the organization is not greatly committed to training and development and sees it as a cost rather than 'adding value' to the human resource. This negative view of training can happen for a number of reasons. But first, I want to clarify two terms that are going to be used throughout:

**Customer**  this can be the individual learner or the organization that employs that learner.

**Product**  this can be a training programme, course or any other learning event or intervention used by the customer and delivered or provided by you or your training unit.

The customer, in this case the individual learner, may view the product negatively because of issues of quality. Poor delivery, poor quality materials, inappropriate delivery methods, inappropriate environment, etc, can all contribute to this. These issues were dealt with comprehensively in chapters 4 (p. 62) and 5 (p. 80).

This chapter focuses on the issue of the *relevance* of the product and this relevance can be identified in Figure 6.1. It can also be identified on two levels, actual relevance and perceived relevance.

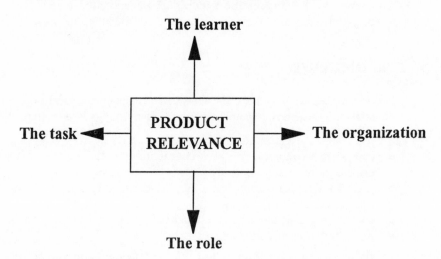

**Figure 6.1**  *Product relevance*

**Actual relevance** This is where the customer recognizes and understands and accepts the need for the product based on factual information.

**Perceived relevance**  This is where the customer does not have access to factual information, or enough factual information to make an informed decision about the relevance of the product, and therefore perceives the need, or not, on the basis of their limited understanding of the situation and on previous experience.

This difference between actual and perceived relevance is important as it has major implications for customer involvement and communications, whatever form the product takes. If the product is not seen as relevant then your credibility, the credibility of your unit and ultimately the credibility of the organization is affected.

## ACTIVITY

Identify why training may not be seen as relevant by customers. Classify the issues under *actual* relevance and *perceived* relevance.

In terms of *actual relevance* the following may apply:

● The customer thinks they are performing effectively already.
● They don't believe the training will improve their performance.
● They feel threatened by change and therefore try to avoid it.
● The subject of the training is not seen to be a large, or important, part of their job.
● They've got enough work to do as it is without taking on more or different work.

Whereas the effects on *perceived relevance* may be as a result of:

● Not being aware of upcoming changes in practice, or markets, or health and safety requirements, or government legislation, or technology.
● They have not been consulted about their training and development needs, now or ever.
● Historically, training is something the organization has 'done' to them and therefore hasn't seemed relevant, then or now.
● Training has been seen as a 'jolly', and not to be taken seriously.
● No one has talked to them about why the training is necessary for them, for the development or survival of the organization, for proposed changes in their job or role, or for changes in one or more of the tasks they perform.

These lists are certainly not exhaustive but highlight some of the more common reasons why training is not seen as relevant or necessary.

### Involving the organization

So far we have looked at one of the factors influencing our decision to get involved with the identification of the performance problem and any ensuing training need; the impact of the learner's understanding or perception of the relevance of the product or intervention. Another major factor is the organization's view of the relevance of the intervention. In chapter 2 (p. 25) we looked at the ways in which the culture of an organization can affect all its functions. This is often most readily observed in the way in which the training function is viewed. As mentioned above, some would say the majority of organizations view training as a cost. As a result of this, when organizations wish to cut costs, the training function is often seen to bear a disproportionate reduction in its budget. Indeed, the author is aware of organizations that, in times of recession, have completely closed down their training function.

The question we need to consider is: 'Would they have closed down their sales department or their marketing department so arbitrarily?' The answer is an unequivocal 'No'. Those departments are seen to be essential to the continuation of the organization. The powers that be in the organization are able to see, without any lobbying from the departments in question, why those functions are important to the continued success of the organization.

So why isn't the training function seen to be as essential as any other function within the organization to the successful attainment of the organization's goals?

- Because, in most cases, the training function has not been consulted at any stage during the formulation of those goals.
- Because the training function is seen as a reactive provider of training interventions on the direction of others.
- Because the training function is not seen as contributing directly and tangibly to the effective and efficient functioning of the organization.
- Because, historically, the training function has addressed the symptoms of the problem, identified by others, and not the cause.
- Because training is seen as a necessary evil, when we can afford it.
- Because the training function has a low profile in the organization and is not politically active in acquiring power, prestige and funding.
- Because no one has ever thought of involving the training function in any kind of business planning.
- Because the effects of ceasing to train and develop the workforce are usually not felt for some time.

## ACTIVITY

Using the information above as a guide, identify to what extent your organization involves the training function in its planning. If it doesn't, what could be done to improve the situation?

For the Activity exercise, as well as one or more of the reasons given above, you may have identified some other issues specific to your organization. This could include things such as:

- Being so busy trying to keep the department going on limited resources that you haven't got time for anything else.
- Not having considered the possibility of getting involved.
- Not letting relevant people in the organization know that you could be involved.

So far we have only considered the implications for us as trainers of getting involved in the identification of training needs. Just as we want the organization and the learner to be committed to and motivated towards any intervention we provide, we also need to understand why we should be committed to involvement in the identification of training needs.

However, many texts on the identification of training needs, or, training needs analysis, fail to consider the importance of such involvement for the continuation of the training function, and by default, your job! Hopefully, the previous section has convinced you of at least one good reason for getting involved. Correcting performance problems is the central concern of training needs analysis. Yet it is often the least recognized area of training and development activity. It is also important to remember that effective training is based on clearly identified training needs and that those needs should be closely associated with the performance requirements of the individual and the organization.

As discussed earlier in the chapter, training that is not seen as effective affects your credibility and that of the training function within your organization. Organizations need to maintain and develop their human resource in order to maintain and develop their performance capability and problems occur when a difference is identified between *actual performance* and *desired performance.*

---

DESIRED PERFORMANCE – ACTUAL PERFORMANCE = PROBLEM

---

This applies to the performance of whole organizations, or departments within them as well as to the performance of individual members of staff.

## An organization's performance

Performance problems could involve the overall profitability of the organization in response to the criticism by shareholders; providing a service against identified quality standards, eg meeting targets for response times in the Emergency Services; not fully utilizing technology available; levels of absenteeism across the organization may be unacceptably high; or the staff may be operating below capacity on any other organizational goal or target.

## A department's or unit's performance

It may not be meeting sales targets or quality targets. Production levels may be less than required, or they may not be servicing another department as effectively as they should. Levels of absenteeism specific to that department may be higher than elsewhere or morale may be lower.

## An individual's performance

They may not be meeting individually set targets such as output or sales or quality. They may not be using technology effectively, or at all. Absence records may be particularly high, or morale low, or there may be complaints from other workers. Or they may have been promoted without acknowledging that they require training in a number of different skills. In other words, any individual goal or target that is not being met is a problem.

The above simply gives you an insight into the different levels of problems that may arise and is certainly not exhaustive. The occupational sector an organization belongs to will often affect goals and targets at all levels in a specific way. The biggest barrier however, to identifying performance problems, at any level, is in the setting of objectives.

## WHAT'S IN IT FOR THE ORGANIZATION?

How will carrying out a training needs analysis (TNA) benefit the organization? Why should it invest resources in what can be a large venture? There are a number of reasons why organizations may need to do this and a number of business advantages that can be gained from this investment. One thing that is constant in all our lives is the inevitability of change, and this is even more true for today's organizations. Technological change is growing at an exponential rate in comparison to twenty or thirty years ago. This in turn puts pressure on organizations to adapt and modify their working practices.

Changes in markets often require significant changes in the way an organization does its business. Issues such as Europeanization, globalization, total quality management, customer care, privatization, a green economy, etc, are some of the current business buzz-words.

Changes occur as a result of political pressure, changing legislation or a more aware customer base, eg, concern over the environment or our health can affect our choice of service or product as we become more demanding. Government departments may enforce change indirectly through such mechanisms as the Patient's Charter or well publicized

Codes of Conduct. As these changes are experienced by the organization often it has to change too. For some this can be really significant, for example, the privatization of the industry. This can be seen to affect the organization directly and immediately and often results in highly visible changes in personnel or roles. It is these types of major organizational change that are most often recognized as needing a TNA.

For the majority of organizations, however, the change is less public and therefore less obvious. Often the change takes place incrementally, over a period of time, as the organization struggles to deal with the changes facing it. It is these organizations that are less likely to immediately address TNA. Yet their need is no less urgent than that of the organization going through massive, and public, restructuring.

## ACTIVITY

What are the potential or actual changes facing your organization and how could training needs analysis (TNA) help support those changes?

Depending on the type of change facing the organization, the proximity of the change and the level in the organization that it is affecting, the following benefits can be gained by TNA:

- It enables you to get very clear information from senior management about the exact nature of the change.
- By carrying out a thorough analysis of this information it is possible to begin to identify the people most likely to be affected by the change.
- By identifying the skills already held by groups and individuals.
- By identifying the skills likely to be needed to implement the changes.
- By identifying the 'gaps' between skills required and skills held.
- By identifying the need to make human resource changes, either specialist recruitment, redundancies, lay-offs, re-allocating work or roles, re-training, etc.
- By being able to identify what training needs arise from the analysis and what are non-training needs, eg, recruitment of people, updating of technology.
- By identifying skills absent or in short supply.
- By providing longer term support to the continuation of the organization by ensuring that skill demand and supply matches that required in the short, medium and long term.
- By prioritizing training needs against the needs of the organization, thereby making more effective use of the training and development function.
- By providing relevant skills-based training to meet those needs, again making more effective use of the training and development function.

This list is by no means exhaustive and could also include such issues as improving the level of acceptance of change in the organization through thorough consultation with the workforce. This, in turn, would improve communication and understanding. However, the list does highlight the benefits that TNA can have for the organization. The extent of the benefits will, of course, depend greatly on how the organization is run. As we saw in chapter 2 (p. 22), organizations come in all shapes and sizes. They have different structures and cultures and therefore respond to challenges in different ways, and this has implications for the way the training function is viewed. Another important consideration is the way in which they determine (or not) their business targets.

Some organizations, particularly large, well-established organizations, have clearly identified business or corporate plans that are thoroughly debated in advance of publication. The function of the business plan is to clearly identify to all interested parties where the organization sees itself going over the next one to three years, and, more important, how it sees itself getting there.

This requires the organization to set unambiguous objectives (where it is going) and a plan for implementation (how it is going to get there). This plan for implementation is usually in the form of further objectives, related to the overall objectives but referring to different levels within the organization. The objectives relate to the performance of specific departments, units or individuals.

## ACTIVITY

Using your organization's business plan answer the following questions.

- Does it have performance objectives for the organization?
- Are they clear and unambiguous?
- Does it have an implementation plan?
- Does it identify how it is going to monitor performance?
- Does it indicate what physical resources are required to meet the objectives?
- Does it identify the human resources required?
- Does it name individuals (or roles) responsible for the implementation?
- Does it identify the current 'skill base' within the organization?
- Does it identify the skill base required to meet the identified objectives?
- Does it identify any training or re-training requirements or, how they are to be identified?
- What information does it contain about the development of its human resource to meet the identified objectives?

You may be one of the lucky people in the fortunate position of working for an organization that can answer 'yes' to the majority of the questions asked in the Activity box. However, it is more likely that you work for an organization that operates on a much more *ad hoc* basis. In that case you may have identified fewer 'yes' responses.

If you are in the position of having clearly identified objectives and their requirements then your task of identifying training needs is probably already well established within your organization. However, in the majority of cases the business plan does not go this far. This makes the identification of training needs much more difficult. If your organization does not have a business plan then it can make the realistic identification of training need almost impossible.

So if your organization has not identified in advance potential performance problems what can you do about it?

## ORGANIZATIONAL TRAINING NEEDS ANALYSIS

The following definition of Training Needs Analysis (TNA) is taken from the Manpower Services Commission's *Glossary of Training Terms* (1981):

*An examination of the organization's present and expected operations and the manpower necessary to carry them out, in order to identify the numbers and categories of staff needing to be trained or re-trained. It may also refer to the training needs of an individual to enable him to reach the required standard of performance in his current or future job.*

As you can see from the above definition, the organization's current and expected operations are an essential component of TNA. Without such clear and unambiguous information any attempt at TNA is just, at worst, a shot in the dark and, at best, an informed guess. This is obviously not satisfactory, but do not lose hope as there are a number of ways in which you can improve on the situation, both within your own organization if it is needed, or within a customer's organization if you are a consultant.

Before we move on to look at strategies you can use to gather the information required at organizational level, it seems appropriate to raise the issue of organization versus training and development needs.

Not all problems are directly related to a lack of training or, indeed, a training need. There are problems that may be beyond the control of the organization as they are external factors, for example, suppliers being on strike. There may be problems with the new technology, for example, bugs in the software. The organization may be under pressure from shareholders who expect unrealistically high performance during times of recession, or a public service may not be given sufficient funds to meet targets effectively.

It is important, as trainers and consultants, that we learn to distinguish between those performance problems that can be addressed through training and those that are a result of other, non-training factors. One of the major reasons why it can often be difficult to distinguish a training need from a non-training need is that today's non-training need is tomorrow's training need.

For example: let us suppose that the performance problem is that the organization's profits were lower than those anticipated by the shareholders, thus affecting the return they can expect on their shares. However, the country is in the middle of a recession and the organization has had two major overseas orders cancelled as a result of an international conflict. This problem is not a training need, as the factors affecting the organization's performance are external to the organization.

Where it would become a training need is if, as a result of this fall in market requirements and therefore a fall in demand for that particular product, the organization decided to restructure or develop new products. These changes would then lead to the necessity for a TNA as there are likely to be training needs directly linked to such changes.

## Symptoms and causes

This leads us on to our final consideration before we look at ways of carrying out an organizational TNA: symptoms and causes. It is often of vital importance that we learn to distinguish between the symptoms of a performance problem and its cause. So much of our training resource is wasted dealing with 'knee-jerk' responses to performance problems identified by others. One of the difficulties is that the problem that is identified, and the solution that is proposed (or prescribed), is 'given' to us by managers.

By this I mean that they identify the problem, write out the prescription from a menu available to them and hand it to the training function to dispense and administer. In other words, managers ask '*Where* is the pain?' when they should be asking '*Why* is the pain?'

One of the knock-on effects of this type of approach to needs analysis is that when the prescription does not work as well as expected it is the prescription that is blamed and not the prescriber. Again, it is the training function that is held to be at fault, not that the problem was not accurately identified. This affects our credibility and stops us contributing effectively to the performance of the organization. This is a threat to us.

## ACTIVITY

Think back over training activities you have been involved in. Can you identify any where you suspect that the symptoms were being treated and not the cause?

## Strategies for organizational TNA

The results of an organizational TNA can help senior management to decide where training is most needed and, therefore, where training resources can be best deployed. It also helps to prioritize training needs. An organizational TNA would normally be carried out once a year, alongside the development of the business plan. There are a number of strategies you can use when gathering information about the organization to inform your TNA. The following section looks at the two most common: strengths, weaknesses, opportunities and threats (commonly known as a SWOT analysis) facing the organization, and the use of internally available information, internal data analysis (IDA).

## SWOT

A SWOT analysis looks at both internal and external issues and their potential effect on the organization.

### Strengths

These could include a flexible and well-skilled workforce, a stable market, high motivation, effective management, a high quality rating. They refer to all aspects of the organization; people, technology, products or services, markets, systems and suppliers, etc. In other words, all the things an organization needs to be successful.

### Weaknesses

These are, in effect, the opposite to the strengths outlined above. There may be a weak skill base, poor quality products, a highly fluctuating and competitive market, high levels of absenteeism, unreliable service, etc. In other words, all the things you do not want in an organization.

### Opportunities

What opportunities are there currently facing the organization? It could be the expansion of a service or product base, the development of new technology, or some external recognition such as Investors in People, ISO 9000 or the Queen's Award for Export: anything that can provide the organization with more strength or stability.

### Threats

These could be economic, such as a recession; or political, for example, a war or a change in legislation; or social, such as a decreased demand for your product because it is tested on animals; or technological, eg, equipment becoming outdated and in need of replacement.

## Internal data analysis

Sources of information include the following:

- Information from the business plan, including mission statement, goals and objectives.
- Inventory of the human resources in terms of their demography, ie, age range, sex, length of service, etc.
- Skills inventory giving a breakdown of skills in the specific operating areas of the organization, how many people have the required skills, to what level, etc.
- By referring to organizational climate indicators such as:
  - Absenteeism
  - Accidents
  - Productivity
  - Grievances
  - Discipline
  - Customer feedback
  - Sickness, long and short term
  - Turnover
  - Quality circles
  - Attitude surveys.
- Consultation with managers and supervisors to discuss any perceived changes in systems or practice.
- Financial information, eg, what resources there are and how they are currently employed. Is there a system of cost-control or cost centres? How much will be available for training and development?
- Marketing information, short and long term. Any complaints from customers about products, services, prices, etc?
- Production information. Any changes expected/anticipated? Are levels of production being met, is labour or plant being fully utilized? Any bottle-necks or problems with quality?

This is not an exhaustive list, and each of these sources can be further broken down into more specific sources, for example, specific manpower information or individual analysis sources.

---

## ACTIVITY

Compile a list of questions that you could ask that would give you information about the current human resource situation in your organization.

---

The following are important issues:

1. What is the age structure?
2. Any anticipated retirements?
3. Any anticipated redundancies?
4. What are the staff turnover rates?
5. What are the reward structures?

6. What consultation systems are in operation?
7. What are the sickness rates?
8. What are the disciplinary rates?
9. What are the absence rates?
10. What are the accident rates?
11. Are there any alternative labour practices, eg, job-share, secondment, etc?
12. What performance objectives are there?
13. Are they clearly communicated to staff?
14. What are the roles, jobs, tasks or occupations required by the organization?
15. Does everyone know what they are?
16. To what extent is there flexibility of staff?
17. How are people promoted?
18. How are roles covered in times of absence?

The answers to these questions can produce a massive amount of information, particularly if your organization has never asked for a TNA to be carried out before. One of the skills you need to acquire is the ability to select the information you need in order to provide an effective analysis of the organization's training needs.

There are a number of pitfalls that can confront us as we gain experience in organizational TNA. They include:

- looking backwards rather than forwards;
- not distinguishing between a training and a non-training need;
- uncritical acceptance of needs identified by others in the organization, including senior management;
- not relating needs to the organization's objectives;
- confusing wants with needs;
- incorrectly prioritizing identified needs;
- relying on intuition rather than objective information;
- failing to establish resource constraints;
- failing to gain acceptance for proposals from senior management;
- perceiving TNA to be a low priority role for the training function.

## DEVISING A PLAN

The most effective way of avoiding these pitfalls, however, is to develop a system, appropriate to your organization, for carrying out the analysis. Many factors will affect the structure of your approach. They include the culture of the organization, its location, how it is structured and managed and the type of business it conducts. This is because all organizations are unique and therefore there is no one list of questions that will fit all organizations.

The following set of guidelines, combined with the information preceding this section, can give you a plan for the analysis tailored to your organization and its needs.

## The analysis plan

1. Designate responsibility for carrying out the TNA.
2. Plan what needs to be done to carry out the analysis.
3. Collect the information you require.
4. Analyse the information to identify performance problems and other challenges facing the organization.
5. As a result of (4), collect further detailed information where necessary.
6. Analyse and interpret the information.
7. Identify training priorities and devise a training plan.
8. Report the findings to the organization.
9. Where necessary, modify the training priorities and training plan.
10. Develop an Action Plan with the organization for implementing the results of the TNA.

### *1. Designate responsibility*

Before beginning an organizational TNA it is necessary to decide on the boundaries of, and justification for, the analysis. Factors that influence these include:

- time available;
- people available;
- your knowledge and experience of the organization;
- your credibility within the organization;
- your seniority or position both as a trainer and as an individual;
- likely access to the data you require;
- who makes the decisions about all these issues within the organization;
- the size, range and geographical spread of the organization and the location of the operational units;
- the range of access you have to all functional and operational units in the organization;
- the commitment of senior management to the organizational TNA.

As you can see, all these factors are also crucial when planning the analysis. However, if you do have difficulties of access to certain aspects of the organization, or the organization is not prepared to resource an analysis of the whole organization, it is possible to carry out such an analysis of one or more departments or units that comprise the organization.

It is important to consider that the narrower the focus of the analysis the less likely it is to relate directly to the priorities of the organization as a whole. If the organization is relatively small then it is possible for one person to carry out the analysis, with the support of senior management. However, in a large organization it may be more effective to have a team of people, including some from outside the training department, as a project team can be much more effective at such a large task than an individual could. It can also be important that you involve other specialists in the analysis as you may identify problems other than those that can be helped by training.

## 2. Planning for the analysis

The resources you have available will help to determine the scope of your analysis. The size of the organization and the amount of time you have available will also affect the amount of work you can do.

Once you have identified the resources and the scope of the analysis you can begin to identify your information requirements and the most likely sources of that information. At this stage you need to be realistic about what you can achieve. As you saw earlier in this chapter, you can end up with a veritable mountain of information. The simplest way to avoid such data overload is by being realistic in this planning stage. So, identify what information you want and how you can realistically obtain it. At this stage it is also important to be aware of the politics of the organization as this will affect your access to both people and information. TNA can sometimes be perceived as threatening to individuals and departments within an organization, usually as a result of poor understanding of the aims and objectives of the activity. Overt organizational backing for the analysis may not always improve this situation. It is very much dependent on the culture of the organization.

## 3. Collecting the information

In chapter 8 (p. 171) we briefly look at some ways you could collect information in a consultancy or advisory role. They are the same methods that you can use for gathering information for a TNA. Indeed, as a consultant, you may be carrying out a TNA as part of your brief. Earlier in this chapter we also identified a number of data sources. Examination of these sources for relevant data will be extremely useful during this stage. Other methods include questioning significant people or groups of people within the organization about their experiences and understanding of the current and future situation.

It is also possible to add to your understanding of the organization, especially a large organization with many functional areas, by observation. Observation of the people, the practices and the general working environment. It can also put some of the information you gather by interviewing into a practical context, by seeing people and departments 'at work'. Using a combination of these methods will help you sort out opinion from fact by providing supporting evidence from a number of different sources. This can help you check the 'facts' of the situation.

Again, the culture of the organization will affect your access to information and also the responses from those people that you interview. If you can stress the confidentiality of the information and the secure aspect of the record keeping process this may help. But be aware of the bias the culture could potentially give to your information.

## 4. Analysing the information

This is perhaps the most difficult aspect of TNA, identifying the problems, searching for causes rather than just accepting symptoms at face value. This will also depend greatly on your skill and your previous experience of TNA. It is at this stage that possible performance problems appear. They can be problems of skill and competence, or they may be issues such as customer care or quality. It is also important to distinguish between those problems that can be resolved through training and development and those that cannot.

Performance problems can be either group-based or of an individual nature. Later in the chapter we examine, in more detail, identification of individual training needs through performance appraisal etc. Group problems, however, are usually structural in origin in that they are closely linked to the organization structure, including the management structure and predominant management style.

Challenges facing the organization are usually identified within the business plan and senior management are likely to be aware of them. The most common problem encountered here is in the way such challenges, and their implications, are communicated throughout the rest of the organization. By bringing together these challenges under the auspices of the TNA the organization can begin to prepare for them.

## 5. Further information requirements

As a result of your findings you may decide that you need to obtain further information, for example, to help you determine the cause of the symptoms you have identified as performance problems. This is especially likely in organizations that are run according to functions, eg, personnel, marketing, production, stores, etc, where a problem in production, such as not meeting daily targets, may actually be due to a problem with stores not supplying on time or suppliers making late or incomplete deliveries. Only by investigating further can you get to the cause of the problem.

Further investigation may also be required to support your original findings, eg, to find another source of evidence to confirm the need you have identified. An example of this could be consulting with supervisors or managers about some of the issues raised during your investigation in order to gain more understanding of the problem. Further investigation should allow you to clearly describe the problem. This is essential if you are to formulate a training plan.

## 6. Interpreting the information

This will result in the identification of the training need and is one of the most difficult steps in the process. It is at this stage that you can begin to put your proposal together. When you begin to do this it is probably worth consulting, informally, with members of the organization who can give you some feedback about the acceptability of the proposals.

This is important for a number of reasons. It may be that the people you have identified as having a training need don't feel they have one, or that they feel it is not their problem. If this is the case, and the staff concerned are not motivated to develop because of this, then any training intervention concerning them is likely to be unsuccessful. This is where individual training needs analysis strategies can be supportive, but more of that later. What will also become obvious at this stage are those problems that will not be improved by training, that are therefore not a 'training need' but require some other intervention by the organization. These issues can be raised, however, as an addendum to the analysis when you report back to the organization.

Stages 7, 8, 9 and 10 are grouped below as they form the 'output' of your analysis, the training plan.

## TRAINING PLANS AND PRIORITIES

It is at this point, where you can clearly articulate your findings from the analysis, that a number of priorities can be identified. Some of these will have a clear training need but they are more likely to be outnumbered by priorities that don't have an immediate training need.

The first thing to do therefore is to draw up a priority list containing both training and non-training needs in order that your recommendations can be effective. If you have identified any system changes, for example, then there is little value in training people before these changes take place as the training will appear out of context. In the list of priorities you need to consider each need in turn and then place them in the order in which they are likely to be most effective.

The priorities will also depend on where the resources can be deployed most effectively. If, as in most organizations, there is a limit to the amount of training and other resources available, then it is important to obtain the maximum from those resources. Value for money is extremely important and you need to highlight the benefits by identifying the 'return on the investment'. This includes cost, time, other resources required and timescale in terms of how soon the benefits will be experienced by the organization.

For example, it might be identified that the senior management require training to prepare them for a change in the status of the organization. One possible solution could be for them to take an MBA course, as this will provide them with a thorough grounding in all aspects of senior management. However, the cost is likely to be in the region of £9,000 per person and the course lasts three years. By this time the organization will have either learned how to cope anyway, or gone out of business.

Alternatives therefore need to be sought and this is where your training expertise becomes very important. With the resources at your disposal you could identify a number of options that you could put to the senior management in the organization in order to address the problem. Using a format similar to that in Figure 6.2 may be useful in helping you prioritize.

| PERFORMANCE PROBLEM IDENTIFIED | TRAINING NEED (implication) | OTHER NEED (implication) | PRIORITY FOR ACTION |
|---|---|---|---|
|  |  |  |  |

**Figure 6.2** *Performance problem priorities*

Remember, at this stage you are not attempting to put together a cut and dried list of actions. The temptation is to consider short-term or 'quick-fix' solutions to problems you encounter. Using the medical model again, it is more effective over time to find out what is causing the headaches rather than just prescribing pain-killers. The solution may take longer to treat but once it has been treated you don't need a repeat prescription for pain-killers, which could be causing other damage of their own anyway!

Once you have drawn up your list of priorities you can begin the next stage in the process: drawing up a training plan for the organization and the report that will support your recommendations.

Report writing is covered, in depth, in chapter 8 (p. 159). It is worth reinforcing, however, that the aim of the report is to influence the recipient to accept and act upon your recommendations. If this does not happen then the organizational TNA is likely to have been carried out in vain.

The aim of the training plan is to identify, in detail, the training requirements highlighted during the organizational TNA. It should specify the job or role requiring the intervention, the aims of any training identified against the performance objectives of that job or role, and the form the training should take. It should identify at what level of priority the training need should be placed as well as indicating any action that needs to be taken to facilitate this training and a target date for completion of the intervention.

The training plan can be recorded briefly in a format similar to that in Figure 6.3.

| JOB/ROLE | AIMS OF TRAINING | METHOD | PRIORITY | ACTION TAKEN | TARGET DATE |
|---|---|---|---|---|---|
| | | | | | |

**Figure 6.3** *Organizational training plan*

The full results of the organizational TNA should be submitted in report form, as identified earlier, with the performance problem priority list and the training plan forming the basis of the report. It is also customary, before submission of the final report, to make a formal presentation of your findings to the senior management of the organization.

This has a number of advantages. It will:

- give you the opportunity to 'sell' your recommendations face-to-face;
- ensure that your eventual report will be read as you will have already generated interest in its contents;
- allow you to discuss your findings and negotiate agreement on points of disagreement or conflict;
- allow you to 'test the water' before committing yourself to paper;
- enable you to gain verbal commitment and support for implementing the findings;
- enable you to identify and negotiate resources more effectively face-to-face;
- ensure that your final report will be viewed more positively as the decision-makers are more likely to feel they have some ownership in its findings if they have had an opportunity to discuss and negotiate the issues with you first.

## INDIVIDUAL TRAINING NEEDS ANALYSIS

In some organizations this is a well-established procedure that takes place at least annually. If this happens in your organization it will help you significantly when you carry out an organizational TNA, as you will have a relatively up-to-date skills audit of the workforce as a result of this process.

This is generally not a process that you are directly involved in, unless you are also a line manager, as individual performance appraisal, the most common form of individual TNA, normally involves the individual and their line manager. You would be available as facilitator in this process, to resolve any differences in perception or to clarify whether the performance problem could be resolved by training. You would not normally assess the individual's performance in the workplace as this is a matter of job-specific expertise.

### Performance appraisal

This normally takes place on an annual basis between an individual and their line manager. It could be described as the process by which an individual's performance in their job or role is assessed and any development needs are identified. One of the most important features of performance appraisal is that it takes place through a process of consultation and negotiation with the individual.

For performance appraisal to be effective, however, it is necessary that the individual, and their line manager, have performance objectives against which performance can be measured. Without performance objectives it is difficult to measure performance, as perceptions of jobs, tasks and roles differ greatly, not only between the manager and the individual but also between individuals carrying them out. The introduction of occupational standards, in the form of competence-based outcomes has also made the assessment of individual performance against objectives more accurate, as individual performance indicators can be established for many jobs and roles.

It is also possible to refer to a number of sources of information about the individual in the same way that we are able to access information for organizational TNA. Such sources could include:

- absence records
- accident records
- grievance and disciplinary records
- quality of output or service
- work sampling
- observation of work
- customer complaints
- productivity records

- interviewing individual
- using questionnaires
- performance appraisal
- management coaching
- attitude surveys
- self-reports
- tests of knowledge and understanding
- off-the-job simulations
- assessment centres

As with organizational TNA you can end up with much more data than you can effectively use. But, as we saw at the beginning of this chapter, many learners end up on training courses without any of the above having taken place. It is simply their 'turn' for training.

Another common scenario is for an organization to decide that all its staff are going to receive a particular kind of training, for example, in customer care, whether they need it or not. The staff are not consulted about this, they are not prepared for it and, often, they don't understand the need for it. As a result the training is not as effective as it could be. This has direct implications for relevance. Only by identifying individual training needs within the context of organizational training needs can we begin to ensure that the training need has relevance to the individual and to the organization. This also allows us to target our limited resources much more effectively.

---

## ACTIVITY

What strategies are used in your organization for assessing individual training needs?

---

## Job analysis

One of the most commonly used forms of job analysis is the use of job descriptions. However, if we look at the Manpower Services Commission's *Glossary of Training Terms* (1981) definition of job description:

*A broad statement of the purpose, scope, responsibilities and tasks which constitute a particular job.*

then we can see that a job description may not be specific enough to assist us in identifying performance problems.

Because job descriptions can be so broad they are also open to interpretation and contain many ambiguities. These include:

- what management want the job holder to do;
- what others think the job holder does;
- what others think the job holder should be doing;
- what the job holder does;
- what the job holder says is done;
- what the job holder believes is being done;
- what the previous job holder did;
- what the job holder believes should be done.

Such information therefore is not as objective as it first appears. Depending on whom you ask you will get different answers to the following questions about the same job:

1. What is the purpose of the job?
2. What are the duties and responsibilities of the job?
3. What authority and discretion is there attached to the job?
4. What relationships does the job holder have with others in the organization?

If you are going to use job descriptions to analyse jobs as a basis for identifying training needs, then you also need to ensure that the job description is current. It is surprising how many organizations use job descriptions that have not been reviewed since they were written many years ago.

---

### ACTIVITY

Examine the job descriptions used in your organization. How useful is the information they provide for training purposes? How could it be improved?

---

The usefulness of the job descriptions will depend on many of the factors identified above. However, there are a number of ways in which you can supplement this information based on the job description itself. You can identify:

- how long the job holder has held that position;
- when the analysis was last updated and by whom;
- how many other people are in similar positions in the organization;
- details of any subordinates the person is responsible for and their roles and responsibilities;
- how the job relates to others in the organization;
- to what extent there is any overlap between that job and others in the organization;
- any proposed or likely changes to the job in the short, medium or long term;

- any opportunities for advancement, either vertically or laterally;
- the degree of management supervision the job holder is exposed to;
- the expected duration of the current job description;
- opportunities for reviewing the job description.

## Task analysis

The final component of individual TNA is task analysis. As with performance appraisal, this is not something that you are likely to have direct responsibility for. To effectively carry out task analysis would require you to have all the skills, knowledge and understanding required to carry out the task you are analysing. Also, to a large extent, occupational standards are replacing the need for individual organizations to carry out their own task analyses.

Where the trainer can complement the standards is by providing information on analytical techniques that will help to generate information in a form that can be used to identify any present or potential performance problems. This in turn will help to identify any training needs.

The trainer's role becomes more apparent if we look at the Manpower Services Commission's *Glossary of Training Terms* (1981) definition of Task Analysis.

*A systematic analysis of the behaviour required to carry out a task with a view to identifying areas of difficulty and the appropriate training techniques and learning aids necessary for successful instruction.*

Task analysis can provide quite specialized information for the trainer, therefore, but it is not likely to be used routinely when carrying out TNA as it is obviously a time-consuming and resource-intensive activity. This, in turn, makes it expensive.

## SUMMARY

This chapter began by exploring the reasons why trainers should get involved in the process of organizational training needs analysis and the benefits, both for the trainer and the organization. After looking at the need for relevance we looked at reasons for the organization to carry out an organizational TNA. This led to an in-depth examination of organizational TNA and the importance of distinguishing between symptoms and causes.

The two most common strategies that support organizational TNA were then discussed and sources of information for the analysis were identified, as well as a check-list for clarifying the current human resource situation. A number of pitfalls that can confront the trainer were also identified and a strategy or plan for avoiding these was formulated.

We then looked at how we could identify training priorities and devise a training plan. Having identified organizational training needs we then examined how individual training needs could be identified, and discussed the role of performance appraisal, job analysis, and task analysis in this process.

The chapter has therefore examined training needs analysis at both macro and micro level and has attempted to equip you with the skills, knowledge and understanding to operate effectively in the domain of training needs analysis.

## References

Manpower Services Commission (1981) *Glossary of Training Terms*, MSC, HMSO, London.

## Further useful reading

Applegarth, M (1991) *How to Take a Training Audit*, Kogan Page, London.

Boydell, T H (1992) *Guide to the Identification of Training Needs*, BACIE, London.

Harrison, R (1992) *Employee Development*, IPM, London. (Chapters 12, 13 and 14.)

Mager, R and Pipe, P (1991) *Analysing Performance Problems*, second edition, Kogan Page, London.

Peterson, R (1992) *Training Needs Analysis in the Workplace*, Kogan Page, London.

Reid, M A, Barrington, F and Kenney, J (1992) *Training Interventions*, third edition, IPM, London. (Chapter 9 gives a more detailed account of the stages of task analysis.)

# 7

## Planning and resourcing

## INTRODUCTION

In chapter 3 (p. 46) we looked at trainer activities that largely took place 'in public'. There are other activities that are essential to the effective performance of today's training professional that take place 'behind closed doors' or 'in the background' and they include planning and organizing the allocation of resources to meet the requirements of the design brief. These include:

- identifying appropriate delivery options;
- working within a clearly identified budget;
- monitoring the use of resources;
- monitoring the performance of training staff involved.

These activities are described as 'behind closed doors' as this is the part of the training professional's role that is rarely seen by others. Our customers see the training need being identified and participate in the development of the design brief. The next thing they are likely to see is the intervention itself. What they have not seen are the processes you go through to put the design brief into practice.

This chapter addresses those 'back-room' activities, both on a macro level (how it all relates to the demands or constraints imposed by the organization) and on a micro level (the requirements of individual design briefs, the people they are intended for and the resources available). We begin by looking at how to develop a strategic training plan, how a training policy is constructed and the role you can play in this area.

We then move on to look at operational planning, how you can address individual training interventions, plans and specifications and how you can prioritize against these demands. This leads us to the identification of appropriate training and development options, choosing methods and media against the identified requirements of the brief. You can then begin to identify the resources (physical and human) required to support these requirements. Allocating, monitoring and supporting resources comes next, and once you have been able to identify, more or less accurately, what the brief requires, we examine the construction of a training budget.

We conclude with an examination of the implications of change and how you can plan to best effect for changes both in the organization and in training and development practice.

## THE TRAINING POLICY

All forward-thinking organizations have a training policy of some kind, as it is essential for the planning and implementation of training and development. Without a training policy it is very difficult to establish a rationale for the development of human resources within the organization. Training policies are developed for a number of reasons and these include to:

- identify the relationship between the organization's objectives (usually in the corporate or business plan) and the training function;
- establish and define the organization's commitment to the training function in the light of its objectives;
- provide operational guidelines for managers for both the planning and implementing of training and the allocation of resources;
- raise the awareness of employees by informing them of the commitment of the organization to their training and development and by clearly stating the opportunities available to them;
- identify who has overall responsibility for training;
- specify the training and development framework of the organization;
- identify and regulate working relationships within training and development;
- enable consistency in training and development across the organization;
- publish a clear, accessible and forward-looking document to guide implementation.

In some less progressive organizations you may not even have a training policy, in which case the rest of this section will be useful in identifying how you can begin the process of developing a policy. If you currently work in an organization that has a training policy but you have no formal input to it, then this section will help you identify how you can become more actively involved. By understanding how a policy can be determined and the form it should take, you can more widely influence and contribute to the training and development strategy of your organization.

A training policy should contain the following features:

1. The role of the training function within the organization.
2. A named senior manager who has responsibility for monitoring and implementing the policy.
3. Clearly identified responsibilities of line managers and supervisors with regard to training and development.
4. Details of support for further and higher education programmes or courses.

5. Details of commitment to continuous professional development.
6. Support for formal qualifications.
7. Arrangements for induction of new employees.
8. Clearly identified arrangements for initial job training.
9. Mechanisms for reviewing individual performance.
10. The organization's commitment to and support for self-development while recognizing the individual's responsibility for this.
11. A reinforcement of the organization's equal opportunities commitment in the context of training and development.

As you can see, this is quite a complex document requiring a strategic look at the organization and its goals. It also requires up-to-date information on current and future trends in training and development. A training policy, therefore, is a marriage between the needs, goals and objectives of the organization and current training and development practice. There are a number of factors, both internal and external to the organization, that may affect specific details within the training policy (see the Activity box).

## ACTIVITY

Identify factors in your organization that may affect your training policy.

Your answers to the Activity exercise could include:

- the products or services you offer;
- the training experiences of your managers;
- the organization's economic, social and environmental objectives;
- the size of the organization;
- the organization's culture;
- previous training policies and practices;
- senior management views of training and development;
- the occupational areas employed by the organization and any professional requirement for updating (or continuation) training;
- the availability of information with regard to the organization's training needs;
- the resources available;
- union and employee expectations;
- the availability of the skills required in the labour market;
- the impact of current or proposed legislation;
- any apprenticeship or government-sponsored training scheme requirements;
- skills held by training staff.

## Demand- versus supply-led training

A further look at the list will show that some of the factors affecting the strategic plan are supply-led and others are demand-led. *Demand-led* means responding to requirements, for example, legislation, union and employee expectations, the need for professional updating. In other words, they are being demanded or asked for. *Supply-led* means that these are the training and development options the organization wants to provide, and will include issues like the existing skills of the trainers, the experience of the training managers, and the resources held by the organization. In other words, there is no immediate demand for this type of intervention but the organization is going to supply it anyway as it feels there is a need for it, or because historically it has always provided this.

So, for example, an organization may have always offered a number of courses to its employees such as report writing, delegation, presentation skills, leadership, etc, and continues to do this on a yearly basis. This is supply-led. Up-and-coming legislation may mean that all employees must be trained in basic food hygiene in order to serve in its shops or they will be breaking the law. This is demand-led.

## Your influence on the training policy

Even if you are not directly involved in the working group which sets up the training policy there are many ways in which you can directly influence various parts of the policy. If you consider the list of influences on an organization's training and development policy, you have an input to many of them by identifying the impact of these issues.

By raising the issues in meetings, by writing reports and making presentations you will be able to bring these issues to the attention of senior management responsible for the development, monitoring and implementation of the training policy.

## THE TRAINING PLAN

The training policy then forms the basis of the strategic plan for training and development in the organization. It enables the senior managers in the organization to prioritize training and development needs against the aims and objectives of the organization. Without a training policy it is very difficult to prioritize needs across an organization as there will be no clearly identified criteria against which to judge the needs of particular sections, departments or functions. Organizations can also be taken by surprise by training needs not budgeted for, for example, the introduction of new equipment or the effects of legislation.

If a training plan is clearly identified and relates directly to the corporate plan, and an organizational training needs analysis is carried out, then there should be no operational surprises. The strategic training plan is not cast in concrete, however, and needs to be able to respond to unplanned changes that occur or unexpected decisions that are made with regard to the operation or its systems within the organization, eg, following Investors in People or the need to introduce new computerized ordering systems or recording systems.

The training plan will consider all requests made or areas for development identified as a result of the organizational training needs analysis and individual training needs analysis. These requests will then be evaluated against the criteria laid down by the training policy and the demands identified by the corporate or business plan. At this stage some demands will be rejected as either not appropriate for the development of the organization (eg, a junior manager wanting day release to do an MBA) or not in line with the training policy (eg, a senior manager wanting block release to do an MBA when the training policy states that no employee will be given block release).

Once a list of both supply- and demand-led training and development requirements are drawn up the process of prioritizing them can begin. All organizations will have a limit to their training and development budget and therefore it is usually not possible to meet all requirements. It is therefore important to prioritize these requirements against the needs of the organization. Once a schedule of priorities is drawn up the next stage in the process can begin: developing operational plans for each of the requirements.

## ACTIVITY

Identify the role you play in developing your organization's training policy. What issues do you influence and what strategies do you use to accomplish this?

## OPERATIONAL PLANNING

The strategic training plan is the overall plan for training and development in the organization and, as such, it deals in general needs identified against the corporate or business plan of the organization. The operational plan converts the strategic plan into a series of specific actions that can be easily identified, implemented and monitored. The operational plan converts the general into the specific. It does this by identifying the factors illustrated in Figure 7.1.

The operational plan in the box (p. 131) represents a hypothetical, prioritized training need. The need identified is management development for junior managers in the organization.

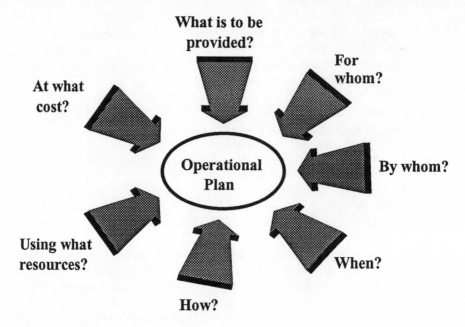

**Figure 7.1** *Factors affecting the operational plan*

The plan raises a number of issues you need to consider. The questions below, under the operational plan headings, will help you explore the range of options available to you.

## By whom?

- Do you have the expertise in-house?
- What level is the programme aimed at?
- How can it be made as relevant as possible to the candidates?
- Is there anyone else in the organization who could contribute?
- Should we/could we invite outside experts to either provide expertise not held within the organization, or to give the programme greater credibility in the perception of the candidates?
- If we don't have much expertise in-house do we sub-contract the programme to an outside organization?
- Do we have sufficient human resources in the training department to cope with this programme? If not, do we take on more staff, full- or part-time, or sub-contract?

## When?

- How many staff are there?
- When can they be released?
- How many at a time?
- Do we need to provide cover for any of these staff?
- How soon do they need to acquire the skills?
- How quickly can the programme be accomplished?

OPERATIONAL PLAN

**What is to be provided?**   Management development training for junior managers.

**For whom?**   For all junior managers in the organization (approximately 30).

**By whom?**   By the training department, senior managers/directors in the organization and appropriate outside experts.

**When?**   Beginning in September 1995. One day a week for 20 weeks and a 3-day residential weekend. Total of 23 days.

**How?**   By a combination of in-house development and delivery using trainers, senior managers/directors and outside experts and a residential period of approximately 3 days to develop teambuilding and leadership skills.

**Using what resources?**   In order to provide manageable group sizes and also to ensure cover at all times it is proposed to run two groups of managers at different times. These resources therefore are × 2.

| | |
|---|---|
| *Training room* | *Photocopier access* |
| *Syndicate room* | *1 Trainer for 23 days* |
| *Flipcharts/OHP/Screen* | *Senior managers' time* |
| *Experts for some topics* | *Administration* |
| *1 Trainer for 3 days (residential)* | |
| *Accommodation for 17 people for 2 nights* | |
| *Video camera, play-back machine and TV* | |

There will also be some one-off costs such as development time for the programme and the purchase of instructional and educational video tapes if they are identified as necessary during the design stage of the programme. (Consider hiring these.)

**At what cost?**   In this section you would insert the costs calculated through the process identified later in this chapter. Indicate both cost per delegate and cost per programme.

- What are the options available? Day-release, a series of short block-releases, whole block-release, evenings, weekends, distance or open learning with workshops? Residential, non-residential, part-residential?
- What is the potential impact on the organization of each of these options?

## How?

- How long is the programme?
- What format is it likely to take, eg, day-release, workshops?
- What were the answers to the *who* questions?
- What media do you have access to?
- What facilities do you have access to?

- Whom is the programme aimed at?
- Will a residential period be potentially beneficial?

## Using what resources?

Many of the options here will depend on answers to some of the previous questions.

- What facilities do you have access to?
- What physical resources do you have or can get access to?
- What arrangements/capacity does the organization have for administrative support?
- How much development/lead time are you likely to have?
- Do you have any 'off-the-shelf' packages available?
- Is there any budget to buy resources you don't already have?

## At what cost?

Although this comes last in the operational plan it is the one factor that informs all the options identified. Cost therefore is often the overriding consideration when identifying and evaluating options for implementing the strategic plan.

All the above criteria need to be considered when evaluating options relevant to the strategic plan and it follows from this that the option(s) selected are those that have the greatest potential for success. By taking account of current operational priorities and needs within the organization the opportunities for success are enhanced.

Once options have been identified, evaluated and selected, agreement needs to be reached with the customer. The plan may be presented orally or in written form. Once agreement has been reached the plan needs to be made available to the relevant people within the organization.

---

## ACTIVITY

Draw up an operational plan for an identified organizational training need.

---

## PLANNING AND AGREEING A TRAINING AND DEVELOPMENT BUDGET

This is of central importance to the operational plan, and often the part most trainers dislike. They see developing a budget as some extremely difficult, mystical process that requires higher level mathematical skills to be successful. In this section I hope to be able to show you that this is not the case.

Developing a training and development budget is a simple procedure once you understand the basic rules. In this case it is a simple calculation to work out the cost of a trainer day, plus knowing what other costs to include.

We will also be looking at direct and indirect costs, although indirect costs are not usually identified for the purposes of an operational plan budget. They are, however, a useful indicator of the 'true' costs of training. Many organizations do not take the final step of costing training and development interventions but simply allocate a pool of money to the organization, or the department, or the unit, and any training needs identified throughout the year have to be met from that pool of money. This often results in a mad scramble for money at the beginning of the year and the subsequent lack of funds if a training need is identified later in the year. (See the Activity box.)

---

## ACTIVITY

What are the benefits of having a clearly defined training budget?

---

Answers to the Activity exercise should include:

1. Fair allocation of funds can be made.
2. Allocation of resources in line with the organization's priorities.
3. Training and development can be more effectively planned.
4. Comparisons can be made between different options.
5. You can justify how the money was spent.

In the not too distant past budgets were often only allocated at departmental level. As organizations have become more efficiency- and quality-conscious, programme budgets are increasingly being allocated against a master training and development budget. It is essential therefore that these programme budgets are accurate and reflect the true costs of the programme.

Also, there is a shift towards individual programmes becoming cost-centres, that is, becoming responsible for the budget for that particular programme. It is essential therefore that trainers develop budgeting skills in the context of training interventions.

More important, in terms of the development of the operational plan, the ability to develop a budget for each of the potential options being explored for the plan allows an accurate comparison to be made. This is particularly important if you need to 'sell' your recommendations to the customer. By having accurate cost comparisons you can provide decision-makers with the quantitative data on which you have based your recommendations. Remember though, cost is not the only criterion, your recommendation must also be in line with the training policy or strategic plan.

The first step in the process is to calculate the cost of the in-house training department or unit (see the Activity box).

---

## ACTIVITY

List the possible costs incurred in a training and development unit/department.

---

These are some of the items you may have listed in your Activity exercise:

- trainers
- administrators/clerical staff
- overheads
- rent/rates
- accommodation

- upkeep of training rooms
- heating/lighting
- telephone/postal
- printing
- photocopying
- computer equipment

They can be broadly grouped into three categories, human resources, physical resources, and systems costs. By identifying the salaries of the human resources, the proportionate costs of the physical resources and, providing there have been no great changes in the system, last year's system costs plus an increase for inflation, it is possible to break the figures down, as shown in the box below, and reach a total for the annual running costs.

| Human resources | £ |
|---|---|
| 3 × trainers (includes NI and superannuation, etc) | 50,000 |
| 1 × admin/clerical | 12,000 |
| **Physical resources** | 6,000 |
| **Systems** | 4,000 |
| **Total annual running costs** | 72,000 |

This figure is important as it allows us to calculate the cost of a trainer day. This is the next step in the process. Calculating the cost of a trainer day is a simple and straightforward exercise. We simply take the total annual running cost and divide it by the total number of days worked by the trainers.

In the example shown there are 3 trainers, and after holidays, etc, they each work 240 days a year. In total, therefore, they work 3 × 240 days, that is, 720 days. The cost per trainer day therefore is £72,000/720. This gives us a daily cost of £100. A trainer day therefore is the overhead cost of a trainer for one day, It does not take into consideration the cost of materials, outside speakers, specialist resources, etc. It is simply the overhead cost of having a trainer.

What is the cost of a training day? A training day involves much more than just having a trainer available, and the cost of a programme is more than just the sum of the cost of a number of training days. To go back to the example earlier in the chapter concerning a junior manager development programme: the trainer requirements were 1 trainer for 23 days and 1 trainer for 3 days, a total of 26 training days. At the cost identified above, £100/trainer day that would equal £2,600 for one programme. There were many other resources identified alongside trainer requirements and these costs need to be calculated.

They will include the costs of video tapes, acetates for overheads, development costs for the programme, any pre-recorded videos needed to buy or hire, books or 'off-the-shelf' materials, etc. For some of these items there will be a 'one-off' cost, for example, development costs. You can calculate the cost per programme by dividing the initial cost by the number of programmes to be run. For the management development programme you could estimate the development cost at 6 trainer days, that is, £600. It is proposed to run 3 programmes this year, the cost per programme therefore is £600/3, that is, £200.

Adding all these costs together will give you a cost per programme. In some organizations there is no direct training budget allocated and funds are therefore included in departmental budgets. In that case you will need to charge the departments which send delegates to the programme. In order to do this you will need to calculate a cost per delegate.

For the management development programme you may have totalled up the costs and reached a figure of £6,000 for each programme. If there are 15 delegates per programme you divide £6,000 by 15. The cost per delegate for the whole programme therefore is £400. You are now in the position where you can compare this cost with the cost of an external programme, as the organizers of these will probably quote you an all-inclusive price per delegate. If you are an external provider or consultant you will also need to build into this cost your profit margin.

The costs all identified so far are *direct* costs, that is, they are directly related to the training intervention. There are other costs attached to training that are generally not referred to as they make the cost appear prohibitively expensive. These are the *indirect* costs and they include such things as the salary costs of the delegates, loss of output or managerial capacity due to the delegates' absence, replacement costs such as overtime paid to other staff to cover for absent staff, a temporary drop in output as new skills are incorporated into existing practice. It is extremely difficult to quantify many of these indirect costs and therefore it is also difficult to cost them. It is important, however, that the trainer developing the budget is aware that these costs exist and can justify them if questioned by the customer.

**ACTIVITY**

Using a training and development programme you are involved in or are familiar with draw up a training and development budget for it. Calculate both the cost per programme and the cost per delegate. Show your calculations for each of the stages in the process.

## OPTIONS AND RESOURCES

One of the key stages in the development of the operational plan is identifying the training and development options available to satisfy the identified objectives. Each option then needs to be evaluated against criteria specific to that need. This is an extremely important stage in the process, as a poor choice at this stage could have disastrous effects on the learner, their manager, the trainer and the training function itself.

Resource implications also need to be considered when the decision is made, as they could be financially disastrous for the organization or the training function or (and more important perhaps), could lead to the rationale for the training intervention being rejected completely by the customer.

**ACTIVITY**

Using your knowledge of training interventions you are or have been involved in identify some of the criteria you or the person responsible for choosing the option may have used to make your/their decision.

Some of the more common criteria for choosing options are:

### Relevance to the workplace

If the option does not seem to have much relevance to the candidates' 'normal' job then this could affect their motivation to learn or develop from it.

### Transferability of skills or knowledge

This is related to relevance to the workplace. If the information or skills are not developed in the context of 'normal' work roles and then followed up in the workplace then this could seriously affect the extent to which the skills can be transferred.

### 'In-house' or 'external'?

Should or could the training intervention be delivered in-house or should an external provider or facilities be used? This, in itself, will depend on a number of criteria. Whom is the training for? If it is assertiveness training for managers should an external consultant be used or would a member of the existing training function be just as effective? This will often depend on the culture of the organization. But it is usual when senior managers are involved in any kind of interpersonal skills training to choose the external option, as it is less sensitive to the politics of the situation.

Still on the theme of in-house or external is the question of the expertise of existing training staff. It may be that external consultants must be employed for this particular intervention if the expertise is not held in-house. This may be for part or the whole of a programme.

This leads to a further choice under this consideration: should it be delivered on the organization's premises or at the expert's premises, or in a hired venue? This again will depend on a number of criteria. Does the organization have the physical resources to deliver the training on their premises? This does not only mean the space to hold the programme but also any equipment that is required. Would holding the training intervention on the organization's premises be detrimental to the learning experience of the candidates, ie, would there be interruptions or would the candidates return to their work during breaks etc?

### The duration

If the intervention leads to a locally or nationally recognized award, the length of the programme is sometimes pre-determined but this is not always the case. Some of the factors affecting your choice in this situation may be the cost, the urgency with which the organization needs to have the candidates develop the knowledge or skills and, also, the knowledge or skills to be acquired. For example, it is very unlikely that a one-day assertiveness programme would lead to any significant development in the skills required for assertive behaviour.

### The commencement date

This again will depend on the urgency with which the organization requires the knowledge or skills to be acquired. It will also depend on the current capacity of the training function and/or the ease with which the new programme or intervention may be accommodated. If the intervention is urgent this may also contribute to the involvement of external experts or an external venue.

### The format

Possible formats include day-release, part day and part evening, a series of one or two day workshops, full block-release, a series of one or two week block-releases, open or distance learning with additional workshops. Any of the above may also have a residential component and some may even be wholly residential, depending on the programme. The format will also have an impact on the course and will often influence the commencement date.

The choice of format will depend on a number of factors including the potential for releasing the candidate from the workplace, the skills or knowledge to be acquired or developed, and outside parameters such as the laid down requirements of a college course, as well as any indirect costs incurred.

Sometimes the cheapest option is not the most practical, however, and it is important therefore that you explore all the criteria relating to the operational plan before making a decision. By exploring all these options you will be able to provide a well-reasoned proposal to support your choice of option.

Once you have agreed the option with the customer the next stage in an in-house programme is to decide on the specific methods and media to be used during the programme. Once you have done this you will be in a position to identify the human and physical resources and the systems required to support that option.

## Methods and media

The methods you choose will most probably determine the media you use and will usually be influenced by the skills and knowledge to be developed by the training intervention. Chapter 5 (p. 80) looked briefly at on-the-job and off-the-job strategies. This chapter broadens the range of options available to support training interventions. Of course, a training intervention usually uses a combination of methods in order to provide a challenging and effective learning environment and also to provide the most appropriate environment for the subject. The factors that influence your choice and therefore have an impact on your resourcing of the programme include:

- the training facilities;
- the equipment available;
- any technology required;
- the skills and knowledge to be developed;
- the culture of the organization;
- the learning styles of the candidates;
- whether an existing programme is available;
- budget;
- expertise held within the organization;
- how it is to be assessed;
- requirements identified by an examining body;
- to give the programme credibility (eg, involving managers or experts).

---

## ACTIVITY

Choose a training intervention you are familiar with or have responsibility for. Identify the factors that have influenced the methods used during the programme and the reasons for their choice.

---

## IDENTIFYING OPTIONS AND RESOURCES

Earlier in the chapter we briefly looked at the different categories of resources required to support a training intervention. This section looks at those resources in more detail.

Human resources include administrative or clerical support, trainers, and any other person involved in the delivery of the programme, such as managers and experts or outside consultants. It also includes support staff, for example, if using an outdoor development facility.

Physical resources include rooms required (will you need 1 or 2 training rooms, any syndicate, rooms, etc?), use of residential premises, CCTV and video and television facilities, purchase of any video or audio tapes (blank or pre-recorded), any supporting resources such as workbooks, files, off-the-shelf training packages, interactive video or computer-based training packages.

They also include refreshment facilities as well as transport if the training programme is off-site, course materials including handouts, manuals, log books, assessment packages, OHP/s and acetates, flip charts, whiteboards plus any development costs where necessary. They may also include the use of any disposable materials such as bandages, fuel, paper, computer disks or paper, or the use of any fixed resources such as computers, vehicles or demonstration equipment.

Systems include assessment systems, recording systems, financial monitoring systems, accreditation systems, management information and quality systems. They also include systems for identifying training needs, allocating places on the programme and any follow up systems required. Most of these systems are the province of the administrator. Other systems include costs such as postage, telephone, printing and photocopying, registering of delegates with awarding bodies, arranging food and accommodation, booking rented facilities and co-ordinating booking of and payments to external speakers or consultants.

None of these categories is exhaustive and the more specialized the training intervention the greater the likelihood of identifying some resource not included above. The lists above, however, should give you a general guide to the kinds of resources required by a training intervention.

Some decisions about resources may be made for you if you choose an externally provided programme, others may be partially decided if you 'buy-in' or modify an existing package. Awarding bodies may specify certain resource requirements and this will have resourcing implications for the option identified in the operational plan.

Once you have identified the resources required for the training intervention you will need to assess the capacity of the organization to provide them. In the areas of physical resources and systems this may be straightforward. However, in order to be able to evaluate the capacity of the human resources required, a further step needs to be taken: drawing up role specifications.

## Drawing up role specifications

Drawing up role specifications for contributors to a training intervention is a straightforward procedure. The first step is to identify *what* you want from the contributors, in other words, *how* you want them to contribute to the programme. Do you want them to co-ordinate it, facilitate it, provide trainer support to experts, deliver one or more sessions, and on what topic? Do you want them to administer it or give clerical support? Are they to be an expert giving professional credibility to the programme with their knowledge or are they a manager from within the organization giving support and relevance to the programme? The nature of their contribution must be established.

Once you have established *what* you want from the contributors, in other words, their role in the programme or intervention, you can then begin to identify a number of more specific factors that will help you specify more accurately what you require from that particular contributor (see the Activity box).

---

### ACTIVITY

What other factors have you considered when identifying contributors for a programme for which you have responsibility?

---

For the Activity exercise you probably identified a number of factors involved in your decisions and they can be broadly included in the categories identified in Figure 7.2.

### *The outcomes*

Is the purpose of the intervention to inform, change attitudes, change behaviour, increase skill, assess skill or knowledge, increase awareness? Once you have decided on the purpose of the session you can identify the outcomes in more detail. Whatever the purpose it will influence processes and attributes required and, in some cases, the skills.

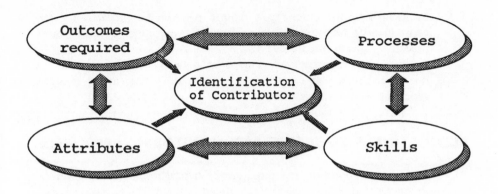

**Figure 7.2** *Factors affecting choice of contributor*

## The processes

Is it to be a demonstration, a lecture, a skills or knowledge test, groupwork, self-assessment, computer-based, facilitated, interactive, didactic, a workshop? Deciding this will help you to identify what skills and attributes you require of the contributor.

## The skills

These will be directly related to the outcomes and processes you have identified. You may require someone with specific expert knowledge who is a competent deliverer of information and can also effectively assess candidates' progress. Or, you may require someone who is competent in certain skills who is effective using groupwork and facilitation techniques. Whatever the outcomes and processes you have identified you will need a contributor who can most effectively combine the two.

## The attributes

Do you require someone who is sympathetic, supportive, assertive, authoritative, cold, warm, understanding, objective, positive, non-committal, patient, confident, able to work under pressure, can manage stress? This will depend on the criteria you have identified under outcomes, processes and skills.

Once you have identified all the criteria you have the beginnings of a role specification. In an ideal world you would be able to identify someone who met all the required criteria. However, this is not an ideal world, so the next step in the process is to identify which of those criteria are essential and which are preferred. In other words, what *must* the contributor have to achieve the desired outcomes and what would it be *nice* if they had as well?

For example, if the only person you find available to deliver a specialist session with expert knowledge is also the worst facilitator you have ever seen, then you may have to re-draw your processes and change the layout of the session to a straightforward lecture and hope for the best. At least by identifying the criteria you require you can be prepared for any consequences. It also makes selection of personnel a much more objective and informed process.

Once the resources and systems have been identified against the operational plan you can move on to the next stage in the process: allocating the resources.

## ALLOCATING, SUPPORTING AND MONITORING RESOURCES

Allocating, supporting and monitoring physical resources is a relatively simple task once they have been identified as part of the operational plan. It is then possible to evaluate the organization's current physical resources capacity. It is important to gain accurate and up-to-date information about the resources available within or to the organization using as many sources as possible. Possible sources of information include technical experts, the training manager, line managers, administrators, colleagues, and documented evidence such as technical manuals or records of resource use and availability.

The physical resources will cover facilities, equipment and materials, and the capacity of current administrative and financial systems will need to be evaluated. Systems are just as important as physical resources but are the most often neglected part of planning a training intervention or development programme. The major reason for this is that it is very difficult to plan the implementation of a programme without allocating rooms, equipment, etc, but too often the assumption is made that the existing administrative system can cope with yet another programme to administer.

If extra resources or systems are required then they need to be budgeted for. It is no good simply assuming that the systems will cope or that resources will be found from somewhere.

## ACTIVITY

Using a training intervention that you are developing or have responsibility for, write an assessment report evaluating the physical resources and systems available to meet the identified training need.

Evaluating the current capacity of human resources to meet the training and development need is a little more complex. Having role specifications as identified in the previous section is the first step in the process. But you also need to identify people who can fulfil that role.

The next step is to identify their current competence in that area, and, if their competence is verified, to evaluate their workload and roles and responsibilities already held. This is more difficult than extracting information about physical resources, since much of the information you require is confidential and as such you will need to adhere to the organization's requirements for confidentiality. This may be more difficult if you are using an external provider or consultant but as they are often in competition for the work they should be able to answer your questions.

There are a number of ways in which you can collect this information. You can speak to human resource professionals in the organization; you can also discuss your requirements with the line manager of the person involved. You can interview, observe their performance in a similar context or analyse written records. Using a combination of these methods will provide you with both qualitative and quantitative data.

Once you have obtained this information and evaluated it against the role specification you can decide on the suitability of the person for the role required. The next step is to report the decision to the relevant person within the organization. You may do this in either oral or written form and you will need to include in your assessment report the reasons for your choice and how you gathered the data on which you based that choice.

## ACTIVITY

Using a programme you are developing or have responsibility for, indicate how you select the contributors to that programme.

## Co-ordinating resources

Co-ordinating physical resources and systems can be relatively straightforward (unless your room is double booked or the video camera is already being used!). With human resources this becomes more complex as more things can go wrong. People fall ill, they are called away to other duties, they forget, or they don't perform adequately. It is very important therefore to develop contingency plans. If you have a contingency plan then the situation can be saved. The plan might simply be to have a series of case-studies available on a specific topic that a group could attempt, or a group project could be set. An available member of the training team could then supervise the process.

Contingencies could also include changes in priorities or need, that is, the need to delay or bring forward the proposed intervention and the effect that this will have on the identified contributors. It may be that not all contributors are available at the changed time and therefore new contributors will need to be identified and selected.

A third kind of change could be a change in format, that is, from day-release to block-release or workshops.

These changes will all have an effect on the contributors. When drawing up your programme plans you will need to identify any contingency plans you propose.

## Supporting contributors

In your role as manager or co-ordinator of the training intervention you have responsibility not only for identifying and allocating the human and physical resources and systems but also to support, co-ordinate and monitor the contributors.

These processes begin once contributors have been identified and allocated to the programme. Contributors should be given a brief that identifies exactly what is required from them in terms of attendance, outcomes, processes and inputs, as well as any evaluation or assessment requirements. By identifying from the start the conditions for their contributions it should be possible to avoid any misconceptions about their role and its requirements.

It is also important at this stage to give the contributors relevant information about the learners. Things like how many, what stage they are at, any special requirements, etc. If contributors are from outside the organization it is also necessary to provide them with other relevant information such as health and safety, security and confidentiality procedures. They should also be informed about the support services available to them, such as administrative services, financial support, access to information and access to facilities and resources such as photocopying, typing, etc.

If there are any last-minute changes to the programme it is essential that *all* contributors are informed and not just those it immediately affects. This provides all contributors with a sense of co-operation and continuity and also avoids any embarrassment when working with the learners if they know the current 'state of play' with the programme.

## PLANNING FOR CHANGE

This section is concerned with the changes that may be required either because of changes in training and development practice, or as a result of programme evaluation (see the Activity box).

## ACTIVITY

Identify changes in training and development practice that have or are likely to affect your work.

These are some common changes that affect current training practice:

- using new training technology;
- changes required by the awarding body;
- changes in the programme syllabus;
- competence-based training and assessment;
- feedback from an external verifier;
- different entry requirements;
- equal opportunities;
- different assessment requirements;
- change of role to adviser/consultant;
- response from customers;
- using Open or Distance learning;
- as a result of your own training and development;
- programme evaluation;
- changes in current practice.

The changes might refer to only a part of a system or to part of the current training intervention but they could also require changes to the whole system or whole programme as a result of evaluation feedback or feedback from external sources.

## ACTIVITY

Using the training interventions that you are or have been involved in as the basis for this activity, identify changes that you have been required to make to the programme and/or its systems and the reasons for these changes.

Once you have identified the reasons for changes then you will be able to consider the alternatives that are available to you. There are usually a number of criteria against which you can judge each of the identified options. They include relevance, practicality and cost. As you saw earlier in this chapter, all training interventions have a cost or a budget and any modifications to be made have to either be within the limits of the existing budget or else attempts need to be made to re-negotiate the budget allocation for that intervention.

For example, if you propose that the intervention requires some input from a specialist where it didn't have any before, then fees will need to be negotiated and costed into the programme.

It is unlikely that the existing budget has already allowed for this expense and therefore either savings will need to be made elsewhere in this budget to accommodate this extra cost, or, if the argument for this change can be supported, then the budget will need to be re-negotiated.

Similarly, if feedback suggests that some sessions during a programme would be more effective if they were double-tutored then the benefits of this must be clearly supported in order to justify the increased cost.

If you identify that the intervention is too short or that there should be a follow-up workshop attached to it, or that a particular video cassette would be useful, or that more printed materials would support it, then you need to be able to clearly identify your rationale for such modifications in order to gain both the support of your programme team for any modifications and also the support of the customer.

Once you have gained commitment to the changes you can draw up an implementation plan and communicate this to all involved.

## The implementation plan

The plan must clearly identify:

1. The improvement(s) to be made.
2. Who is responsible for ensuring the improvements occur.
3. The human resource implications, ie who is required, how they are to be recruited/selected, what their role is to be.
4. The physical resource implications, ie what is required, from where, by when and, where appropriate, at what cost.
5. Any systems implications, along with whose responsibility it is to advise and monitor these changes.
6. The timescale for each stage of the implementation process, as well as a review date for evaluating progress.
7. The monitoring process, and the named individuals responsible for this.
8. The sources of evidence to evaluate the change, in advance where possible. These will probably include training activity evaluations, feedback from the management system, informal discussions with all relevant parties and the results of performance management systems.

Once the plan has been developed it may need to be agreed with the customer and then presented to those people likely to be affected by it.

## SUMMARY

As a result of this chapter you should have developed your skills, knowledge and understanding of strategic and operational planning to meet training and development needs. It should also have developed your competence in putting the operational plan into practice.

Strategic and operational planning is of central importance to the training and development function, as is budgeting. They are, however, ignored by many organizations or paid lip-service to in others. This chapter should therefore have developed your commitment to these practices by allowing you to develop skill in these areas while at the same time developing your understanding of the processes involved and the role you can play. The next step in the process was to identify appropriate training and development options in order to implement the operational plan.

Once the options had been identified we moved on to the next stage, identifying the resources required to support the programme. Following on from this we looked at allocating those resources to the programme and the issues that this raises for you and how to support and monitor those resources. The final consideration was planning for the effects of change and how that could affect the implementation plan and your involvement with it.

## Further useful reading

Harrison, R (1992) *Employee Development*, IPM, London. (Chapters 9 and 10 look at organizing and managing training and development resources, both physical and human.)

Newby, T (1992) *Cost-effective Training*, Kogan Page, London.

Parsloe, E (1992) *Coaching, Mentoring and Assessing, a Practical Guide to Developing Competence*, Kogan Page, London.

Pepper, A D (1987) *Managing the Training and Development Function*, Gower, Aldershot.

Robinson, K (1989) *A Handbook of Training Management*, second edition, Kogan Page, London.

Sheal, P (1994) *How to Develop and Present Staff Training Courses*, second edition, Kogan Page, London.

Stout, S (1992) *Managing Training*, Kogan Page, London.

# 8

# Consulting and advising

## INTRODUCTION

As a trainer, it is very easy to view your role as someone who simply designs and delivers training interventions. This focus on the task is not just confined to trainers, however. Managers see their function as managing, writers as writing, teachers as teaching. We focus on the easily identified demands of the role. However, embedded in all roles are a number of more cross-functional skills. These skills, and the knowledge and understanding that underpins them, can also be referred to as generic competencies, or the things you need to be able to do to do the things you do.

If, as a trainer, your interpersonal skills were in serious need of development, then no matter how much effort you put into developing specific trainer skills, such as writing training outcomes or developing methods of self-assessment, your effectiveness as a trainer, and your competence, would rarely be fully developed. This is because interpersonal skills form an integral part of trainer and developer skills. The following could be described as generic skills:

- record keeping
- report writing
- negotiating
- interviewing
- giving and receiving feedback
- researching information

- presenting information
- running meetings
- contributing to meetings
- counselling
- consulting
- advising

This list is by no means exhaustive but covers the more common generic skills required by a trainer. The focus of this chapter is on the underpinning knowledge required to support the development of these skills. It begins by looking at these skills in a generic context then concludes by applying them to a formal consulting role. One of the difficulties we often face, however, is our underdeveloped ability to recognize informal communication opportunities.

This next section considers in more detail the opportunities you have or can create, for working informally in your organization.

## WORKING INFORMALLY

Why do we need to concern ourselves with working informally within our organizations? Why can't we just get on with what we are getting paid for – delivering training? The answer is a simple one, and was arrived at in chapter 2 (p. 22). You need to be able to work informally in your organization because training does not take place in a vacuum. It occurs because of a series of interactions between departments or sections, sometimes with external organizations, which have identified a performance problem, real or potential, that you are then expected to respond to.

By working informally in your organization you can increase the influence the training function has. You can do this by contributing to the wider decision-making process and also by being able to influence training and interventions at an earlier stage and on a wider scale. It may also enable you to move from simply being a trainer reacting to demands led by other areas of the organization to being more proactive in working alongside your customers.

This is a very important consideration that trainers now need to acknowledge. The more you can put in to the initial decision-making process, ie, the training and development needs analysis, the more you are seen to be able to advise others and be available for their consultation, the more power, influence and, ultimately, credibility you and the training function generally will have. It is also important because it can enable the trainer and the training function to be seen and recognized as an integral part of the organization. This lessens the likelihood of the training function being marginalized in times of recession and internal budgetary cuts.

Informal working is any use of your training and development skills and expertise within your organization that is not part of your formally identified work role. Therefore, if your formal work role is to develop and run courses that your manager has identified for you then working informally could be answering queries that a line manager has about a particular programme, or responding to an informal request for advice about a particular learner or performance problem.

The types of formal and informal activities you may perform will depend on your current job description and identified role, but there are some suggestions below.

1. Responding to a telephone request for information from a line manager or learner.
2. Giving advice on possible solutions to a performance problem.
3. Discussing training issues with people from other departments in the rest room or canteen.
4. Visiting the 'shop-floor' (whatever that is in your organization), to get a feel of what is happening.
5. Responding to written requests for information.
6. Networking with people in other departments to keep each other up

to date with what is happening in each of your spheres of operation.
7. Making observations to your manager about current or future trends within the organization and ways in which you and your department or function could respond.

Some of the above activities could be seen as simply reactive, but if you have made it known that you are available to provide consultation and information then that makes your approach proactive, and that is the key to working informally in your organization.

---

## ACTIVITY

What opportunities do you have for working informally within your organization? How could you develop this further?

---

## GIVING PRESENTATIONS

A training presentation provides learners with specific information that is usually occupation, job, or task-related and they need the information to improve their performance. However, this chapter is more concerned with enabling you to more fully use the opportunities you have, both formally and informally, for consulting, advising, and therefore influencing people other than your direct client group of learners. This is to be the focus of this section on giving presentations. The presentation may be a formal one to a large group of people, or a more informal one to only three or four. Whatever the scenario, however, the focus will be the same: to persuade and influence as well as to inform.

Giving a presentation, particularly to people either at a higher level than you within your organization, or to people from outside your organization, is often something viewed with great trepidation. Few people feel entirely comfortable making a presentation and even fewer actually enjoy it.

The opportunities you have for giving presentations will depend on your current role within your organization. If the opportunities you have are scarce then perhaps you could consider how you could expand or develop your role to accommodate this. It may be a means of increasing the opportunities you have for being proactive within your organization.

Research has shown that most of the things that people commonly dislike about giving presentations either stimulate fear or are the result of fear. Fear of humiliation, embarrassment, loss of self-esteem and dignity. Even the most experienced speakers often feel the symptoms of fear before and during a presentation. The key to success is to make use of that fear. There is nothing wrong with it and it can be a very healthy feeling – if you can learn to harness the very energy it produces to help you perform well.

In order to begin this process, however, you need to identify the fears you have about giving presentations. You need to follow this by identifying your strengths and weaknesses in this area. These are the first steps in making your presentations more effective. Once you have identified the areas that you need to concentrate on and practise, then your energy can be fruitfully diverted into those areas and away from fuelling the often unfocused anxieties that you have.

## ACTIVITY

Think back to two presentations that you have made: one that went really well and one that you feel could have gone considerably better. Using your recollections of those two presentations, identify your strengths and the areas you feel you need to improve.

Once you have identified your fears and your strengths and weaknesses you can begin to explore ways in which you can improve your performance, and thereby negate, to a large extent, your fears. The keys to effective presentation can be seen in Figure 8.1.

## Understanding your audience

Whether your audience is large or small, the presentation formal or informal, there are certain questions you can ask before beginning to plan and prepare your presentation. These questions will help to defuse any fear you have about the audience. It also helps if you remember that your audience is made up of individuals just like you. Most people will feel a natural empathy with you and will want you to succeed. But because we put a considerable amount of effort into preparing for a presentation and because we often view it as our only chance to put across something important, we put tremendous pressure on ourselves to handle everything perfectly.

Either that or we avoid presentations altogether, or, even worse, we rush it all together at the last minute, feel hassled, make a mess of it and tell ourselves 'I told you so!' The easiest way to get over this hurdle therefore is to consider your audience before you begin. The following check-list of questions may help.

1. How many people will be there?
2. Who are they?
3. What are their roles?
4. Do I know any of them?

**Figure 8.1** *Keys to effective presentations*

5. Will they know why I'm there?
6. What are they expecting from the presentation?
7. What do I want to achieve?
8. Am I informing, influencing or persuading them?
9. How interested are the audience likely to be in the topic?
10. What level of knowledge do they have already?
11. Will they be familiar with the 'jargon'?
12. Have they any experience of the topic?
13. Might they have any preconceptions or misconceptions about the topic?
14. How do I want them to respond to the presentation? Feedback or action?
15. Do they respect my knowledge, values and opinions?
16. Is the topic likely to be controversial?

Once you have found out about your audience and their expectations you can move on to the next stage: planning your presentation. If you find that you are unable to satisfy yourself on some of the key issues regarding your audience then now is the time to question why you are actually going to speak to this particular audience.

It may be that you have been pressured into giving the presentation and are not the most appropriate person to take on this responsibility. If you feel this is the case then you need to take steps to resolve the conflict by re-negotiating your position. If you find that this is not possible then you need to be aware of the limitations this puts on your preparation for the presentation.

## Preparing for the presentation

It is unlikely that you will ever have total control over the circumstances surrounding your presentation. You may not be able to influence the seating arrangements or the room layout. You may have no say over the amount of time you are allocated or at what stage on the agenda your presentation is scheduled.

You may find that what you want to achieve is in conflict with what is expected from you: you may be asked specifically to account for poor performance in one area when what you actually want to do is address specifically how that performance could be improved. It would be wonderful if these external factors actually supported your presentation, or at least did not hinder it, but, unfortunately, life is not always that simple.

The following questions can help you establish the purpose and content of your presentation.

1. What is the main purpose of your presentation?
   - to persuade?
   - to inform?
   - to influence?
   - to change things?
2. What is the primary message you want to communicate?
3. What are the main points you need to make to achieve point 2?
4. Do you need supporting information? If yes, where can you get it?
5. How much time do you need and how much are you likely to have?
6. Would it help to give your audience any information in advance?
7. Would using visual aids clarify important points?
8. How can you best anticipate and prepare for questions?
9. Do you need to provide a summary of your presentation for distribution after the event?
10. What do you want the audience to do as a result of the presentation?

Once you have clarified what you want to achieve and what you want to cover you can begin to structure your presentation. Once again, the following questions may help you do this.

1. How can you best use the knowledge you have of your audience to help you decide what to include and at what level?
2. What is the best order for your presentation? What key points do you want to make during the introduction, main body and conclusion of your presentation?

---

## A cautionary note!

If you are experienced in giving presentations in a training context you may have a tendency to take this preparation for granted, or to feel that so far this is simply restating the obvious. It is necessary therefore to reiterate the focus of this chapter. Extending your influence through consulting and advising within your organization requires a different emphasis from your existing skills than the use of such skills to provide learning opportunities. The specific focus for this section on presentation skills therefore is to persuade, to influence and to inform.

---

3.  How can you gain your audience's attention right from the start?
4.  What information do you have to support your argument? Don't overload your audience with information. Put it in a handout if you need to.
5.  How can you link your main points together to form a cohesive argument?
6.  Where in your presentation do you need to summarize?
7.  Does your communication style need to be formal or informal?
8.  What level does your language need to adopt?
9.  What specific visual aids could illustrate your points?
10. How could you best conclude your presentation?

The final aspect you need to consider is the actual delivery of the presentation.

## Delivering the presentation

The method of delivery you choose will depend on your audience, your subject and your level of confidence in your knowledge and material. Whatever method you choose, remember that other people may have less knowledge or understanding of the subject than you but don't wish to be subjected to unnecessary detail.

1.  You may choose to speak from a prepared script. This is useful if you fear 'drying-up' part way through your presentation. One of the disadvantages of this method, however, is that your delivery may appear stilted if you read word for word.
2.  You could choose to speak using key cards. This is where you write down key words or phrases on a small card, which you can refer to to keep you 'on-track' during your presentation. One disadvantage of this method is that you need to be very familiar with your topic.
3.  You could use overhead projector slides to serve the same purpose as key cards. This also serves the dual purpose of keeping the audience's attention focused on your argument.

4. You may choose to give out information in advance, perhaps a synopsis of your key points.

First impressions are important. Don't mumble or rush your words. Make sure your speech tone varies, particularly if you are reading from notes. Control of the audience is also important. You can't maintain eye-contact and read from your notes at the same time! Try not to distract your audience by unnecessary twiddling or fiddling. Pace yourself and keep an eye on the time. It is no good having a wonderfully prepared argument if you run out of time.

Verbally signpost the progression of the presentation to the audience. You can do this by saying such things as:

'The first point I wish to make is . . .'
'Secondly . . .'
'and my final point is . . .'
'If I can just sum up my main points.'

This is all well and good you may say, if I am given sufficient notice of the presentation and if I am given time to prepare. But what about the time when I am dropped into it at the last minute? In a situation of this kind the first rule is *do not panic*! Second, don't ramble. Third, don't undermine yourself by saying something like, 'You'll have to excuse me if I make a mistake because I haven't had time to prepare anything.' They should know that already. Finally, try to get a couple of minutes to gather your thoughts and give you time to write down some key points on a card to help give your presentation some structure.

## ACTIVITY

Using the information provided in this section devise a check-list that could be used to assess your performance in your next presentation.

## MAKING THE MOST OF MEETINGS

Meetings may range from highly formal occasions, complete with chairperson, secretary, agenda, minutes and statutory rules of procedure, to very informal, *ad hoc* meetings between colleagues, informal discussions, or 'corridor meetings'.

Your role within your organization will to a large extent determine the number and kinds of meetings you attend, but they could include some of the following:

● unit;
● management;

- with assessors;
- with external verifiers;
- with employers;
- departmental;
- 'tea-break', with colleagues.

The functions of the meetings could include:

- to gather information;
- to bring together a range of knowledge and experience;
- to give information;
- to take decisions;
- to influence policy;
- to aid problem solving;
- to air grievances;
- to evaluate current activities;
- to allocate resources;
- to assist strategic decision-making;
- to plan.

Whatever your role, meetings are usually an inevitable fact of life. But how do you feel about the meetings you have to attend? You may like meetings, on the other hand, you may dislike meetings because you feel there are too many of them, or that they are boring or a waste of time. There are many benefits to meetings, however. They are the most effective way of involving all relevant parties in the decision-making process. Where they are well planned and well managed they can be the most valuable means of communication within your organization. Benefits include:

- improved horizontal communication between departments;
- increased job satisfaction as you begin to feel that your views actually matter and can influence decisions;
- management can stay informed of the feelings and opinions of their staff;
- you can keep up to date with the latest developments, both throughout the organization as well as across training and development;
- bringing together a breadth of knowledge and experience that are not available in one single person;

- they can result in positive discussion of issues affecting the department, whether this be problem-solving, promoting or managing change or decision-making;
- they can usefully clarify understanding of complex or difficult issues, eg, interpretation of performance criteria or selecting suitable evidence.

So far we have looked at the kinds of meetings you may attend, the reasons for or functions of those meetings, and the benefits meetings may have. What we need to consider also, is *how* you can make the most of your meetings.

Knowing why you are there and what the possible benefits of the meeting are for you is the first step. The next step is to understand what is going on in the meeting. There are three major influences here. The first one is the agenda, the second is the hidden agenda and the third, the participants. The level of satisfaction gained from meetings is related to the extent to which these three areas are satisfied. This is demonstrated in Figure 8.2.

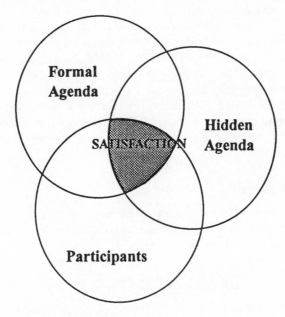

**Figure 8.2** *Factors affecting satisfaction at meetings*

## The agenda

There are usually two agendas at work in a meeting. There is the formal agenda that is usually circulated in advance of the meeting. So why is it that sometimes, as you leave a meeting, you wonder what on earth that meeting had to do with the agenda? Why is it that what should have been a short and fairly straightforward meeting turns into a long, drawn-out and often boring affair? This is because of the second type of agenda, the hidden agenda!

## The hidden agenda

How does the hidden agenda differ from the formal agenda? A formal agenda is written down and usually circulated before the meeting to encourage support and participation from attendees. The hidden agenda, however, is much less easily identified and is not openly stated. The hidden agenda is usually only held by one member of the meeting, which means that every participant could have their own hidden agenda. Only occasionally is there a shared hidden agenda among members with common interests.

The reasons for hidden agendas can usually be traced to organizational politics, with individual members trying to do their best for their unit or department, or even themselves. Formal agendas usually don't allow an opportunity for issues that may have a political impact on the organization; in contrast, the hidden agenda may be essentially political and manipulative.

Making yourself familiar with the hidden agenda can greatly increase your effectiveness within meetings, and what you take away from them as it is likely that you too will have a hidden agenda. The importance of recognizing the hidden agendas in meetings cannot be over-stressed. They can explain many of the subtleties of behaviour that appear to have little to do with the topic under consideration. Yet, through skilful manipulation of the group, hidden agendas may dominate discussions during the meeting, leaving others wondering where the meeting went wrong.

## The participants

Meetings comprise groups of people, and as a trainer you know that putting a number of individuals together to form a group creates all kinds of communication issues. One of the easiest ways to recognize the effects other people at meetings can have on what you get out of the meeting is first, to categorize them, and second, to identify ways of coping with them.

We refer to the behaviours which others exhibit that are counter-productive to the group as selfish-oriented behaviours, and there are a number of readily identifiable types. The following strategies may help.

***Definitely wrong:*** Say, 'I can see your point,' or 'That is one way of looking at it,' but then add, 'Can we apply that to what we are discussing here?' This person needs handling delicately as you want to avoid embarrassing them in front of everyone else.

***Openly argumentative:*** Keep your temper firmly in check and don't let the group get excited. Try to move on to some other point.

***Rambler:*** When they stop for breath, thank them and try and re-focus their attention by summarizing the main points. As a last resort, glance openly at your watch.

***Over-talkative:*** Don't be hostile or sarcastic. Try to slow them down by asking a difficult question and say, 'Let's see what the others think'.

***Will not talk:*** How you cope with this will depend on what is motivating them. You could ask them directly for their opinion. If they are nervous or shy, compliment them the first time they make a contribution.

***Obstinate:*** Throw their view open to the group and encourage them to comment briefly on it.

***Complainer:*** Restate the objective of the discussion and refer to the time pressures on the meeting. Refer them to an alternative audience for their concerns.

***Side conversation:*** Don't embarrass them by ordering them to be quiet. Call one of them by name, restate the last point made and ask for their comments.

As you can see, the above strategies will not only enable you to make the most out of meetings, but are also extremely useful when you have to chair a meeting, or any other sort of group.

## REPORT WRITING AND RECORD KEEPING

These are skills that are called upon quite regularly in your role as a trainer and yet, often, little recognition is given to the fact that we are not born with these skills. There is almost an unspoken expectation that we can do these things, and, if it is so easy, why do we usually find a hundred other things we absolutely must do first!

Unfortunately, avoiding the 'paperwork' aspect of the role does not make it go away. It just looms ever larger. Report writing, however, is quite a straightforward task if you follow some basic rules. These rules do not only apply to writing reports, whether short or long, but also to memos and letters. First you need to look at why you might need to write a report.

Your reports could be on a number of issues:

- responding to a request for information;
- evaluating a programme;
- proposing a solution to a performance problem;
- identifying a performance problem;
- proposing changes to current practice;
- justifying a need for more resources;

- reviewing performance;
- responding to an external client need;
- identifying a gap in the market;
- reviewing changes in practice;
- as a result of a training needs analysis;
- responding to a request from an awarding body;
- a quarterly or annual report on the department's activities.

Whatever the reason for the report, there is a simple strategy for writing you can follow that will make the process much smoother.

1. Decide why you are writing and what you want to achieve and always keep that objective in mind as you write.
2. Remember for whom you are writing it and tailor your style and approach to suit.
3. Have a clear picture before you start of what your readers want. What do they need to know and in how much detail? Your senior manager may just want a summary of progress with some succinct recommendations. The board may require much more detailed information written in less technical language. Remember, however well written, your communication will not be effective if it is not what the recipient requires.
4. If you haven't been given a deadline, set yourself one. Stick to it!
5. Do not feel that you have to write in the order in which the document is to be read. Start where you feel most comfortable. Some people find it easier to start at the end and work backwards.
6. Start writing as soon as you can, even if you throw your first draft out later. Get something down on paper.
7. Start by jotting down some main headings and then brainstorming ideas under each one. You can then put your thoughts in some order before you begin writing sentences and paragraphs.
8. Select an appropriate style and format to suit the purpose of the report and the needs of the recipient.
9. Always read through what you have written and edit it. Is the grammar correct? Are the sentences too long? Does it say what you want it to say? Will it achieve the objective? If you have time it is useful to put the first draft to one side for a couple of days and get on with something else. Coming back after an interval can help you look at the report more objectively.

10. Try to criticize your draft objectively, and, if possible, get a second opinion from a colleague or friend.

## Layout and presentation

Once you have the basic strategy for writing, you can tackle some of the technicalities. Having considered your objective, and your audience, you also need to ensure that the report is accessible. In other words, that the recipients can find their way around it. You might have had a wonderful idea, but if it is lost somewhere in the presentation then its impact is greatly lessened. The following points may assist you:

1. Use a title or heading to make the purpose and content of the document clear.
2. In a long document, use headings and sub-headings to break up the text.
3. Use short sentences and short paragraphs and leave plenty of 'white space' between sections. This makes the document seem less dense.
4. If it is a long or complex document, number your paragraphs.
5. It can be easier to use lists or bullet points to emphasize or summarize information rather than using long, dense paragraphs.
6. If you need to use tables or diagrams to illustrate a point, make sure they are clearly labelled.
7. Use highlighting options such as **bold**, <u>underlining</u>, CAPITALS, *italics*, but use them sparingly and be consistent throughout the document; do not mix them.
8. Use double line spacing if you have a lot of text, or if you are preparing a draft for comment or amendment by others.
9. Use a simple typeface, at least 12 point in size, to make reading easier.
10. Make sure there is enough margin space for binding if necessary. Also, it is useful to leave margin space for the recipients to be able to annotate the report if they wish.
11. If it is a long document, include a table of contents, an introductory summary, and appendices containing detail which might not be of interest to all readers.
12. Present it professionally in a folder.

## Record keeping

It is not possible to cover here all possible aspects of record keeping as there will be differences between organizations and awarding bodies. Many of the recommendations made in the previous section on report writing will also apply to record keeping. The major objective of this section is to simply reinforce the confidential aspect of record keeping.

Whether it is a report of an interview, counselling or otherwise, an assessment report or record, or a summary of the learner's achievement, those records should be stored in a secure place and only authorized personnel should have access to them. If the records are computerized then you must be registered under the Data Protection Act.

If your organization has achieved BS 5750 approval, the Baldridge award, or ISO 9000 then there is very little likelihood of a problem arising. If you do not already have quality systems in place then it is imperative that a safe and secure environment is provided for the storage of such records and that access to them is recorded.

## INTERVIEWING

As a trainer you are probably involved in all kinds of interviews. The focus of this section is therefore on a basic interviewing strategy that can help you across a range of scenarios.

The first part of this section will outline a strategy you can use for preparing for and carrying out the interview. The second part will look at the four major skill groups that are used during the interviewing process: recording information, eliciting information, presenting information and managing the emotional content of the interview. The third part will look at how you can most effectively manage the counselling interview.

### Planning the interview

- decide the objective(s) of the interview;
- prepare a list of topics you want to cover during the interview;
- decide how you will meet the interviewee;
- decide how formal or informal you want the interview to be;
- how are you going to introduce yourself?
- how will you put the interviewee at ease?
- decide where the interview will take place;
- plan the physical layout of the room depending on how formal you have decided to be;
- how are you going to ensure that the interviewee knows, and understands, the purpose of the interview?
- decide how you are going to record the proceedings, and outcome, of the interview;
- decide who, if anyone, also needs to know the interview is taking place.

These basic considerations will help to ensure that both parties are clear about the purpose of the interview and will help to get it off to a positive start.

### Carrying out the interview

#### 1. Put the interviewee at ease

Do not immediately jump into the formal part of the interview. Start by talking about more general things while the interviewee gets used to the environment.

## 2. Explain the objectives of the interview

This should be from the perspective of the interviewee, so explain what the objectives of the interview are for them, not for you. This is important as you should be completely open as to the purpose of the interview. It is immoral to manipulate the interviewee.

## 3. Inform the interviewee about the confidentiality of the meeting

This is important if you are to begin to generate an atmosphere of relaxation, trust and confidence. Without this happening the interview will not be as effective as it could.

## 4. Try to get the interviewee to do the talking

The more time the interviewee spends talking the more you can learn. Unfortunately, in many situations, it is the interviewer who does most of the talking. Remember the 80/20 rule; the interviewer should spend 80 per cent of their time listening and 20 per cent talking. Listening is a skill in itself and may need to be learned.

## 5. Follow up generalized answers

You are usually after quite specific information, especially when you are assessing competence. If the person says something general, such as, 'We always monitor equal opportunities,' follow it up with more probing questions such as:

- Who does?
- How often?
- What methods do you use?
- What do you do if something comes to light?

## 6. Avoid certain types of question

Leading questions, eg, 'How do you feel about this outdated system?'; multiple questions, eg, 'How do you use this system, does it cause you any problems, and, if it does, what do you do about it?', because you can't always tell which question they are answering, and they may miss parts of it out.

## 7. Check that you have understood their response

You can do this by summarizing what they have just said — but not word for word!

## 8. Conclude the interview

Ask if the interviewee wants to ask or tell you anything else. Then summarize what you feel the interview has achieved and what happens next.

## BASIC INTERVIEWING SKILLS

There are a number of basic skills that you can develop to guide you through this step-by-step process and they are discussed in the following sections.

### Recording information

Recording information during an interview is probably one of the more difficult tasks you have to do. If you are using a check-list, then ticking off areas is straightforward. If you need to record responses to specific questions however, then there are a limited number of methods at your disposal.

If you have prepared a list of questions or topics that you want to cover during the interview, you can leave enough space between them to be able to jot down at least the key points of their answers. Or you could simply try to write down everything the interviewee says in response to questions asked and try to sort the sense out of it after the interview.

You can jot down key responses during the interview and write it up fully *immediately* afterwards, or you can audio tape or video record the interview, but only with the interviewee's genuine consent.

Perhaps the best strategy is a combination of the above; use a check-list, jot down key points, write up a longer account immediately after the interview. However, the most important consideration is to gain the interviewee's agreement for whichever methods you use, along with what will happen with the product of that strategy, that is, the written or recorded record of the proceedings.

### Eliciting information

Open questions are very useful for starting a discussion because the interviewee then has a choice as to how to answer. They are also useful for eliciting general information at the beginning of the interview. Once the interviewee has begun to respond to open questions you can probe more deeply to elicit more specific information.

One of the easiest ways to do this is to form them out of the interviewee's own words; for example, 'You said a moment ago that your records are all kept confidential and secure. How do you do this?' If you only ask probing questions it will feel more like an interrogation than an interview and this will restrict the amount of information you elicit. This is also important in terms of the emotional atmosphere created.

Closed questions are useful for checking out assumptions that you may make following an interviewee's response. For example, 'When you said that you observe learners in a group, are you assessing them then?' Closed questions also give you control over the interview. However, if you use a lot of them the interviewee can become frustrated. This is because he/she may not be able to elaborate on things that you ask. Also, if the interviewee is inarticulate, there is a temptation to use closed questions because they make it easier for you and the interviewee. You have to consider if you are being fair to the interviewee by doing this, for it is particularly important if you are questioning underpinning knowledge and understanding, to give the candidate every opportunity to provide evidence of their competence.

Your non-verbal behaviour will also help elicit further information. Nodding, smiling, phrases like, 'Yes, I see,' or 'That's interesting,' will indicate your interest and encourage the interviewee to continue. Summarizing is also a useful skill to have. It can allow you to check that you have correctly interpreted the main points of the discussion and it assures the other person that you have been listening. Figure 8.3 represents the information filtering process that can result from this strategy in order to end up with 'the facts'.

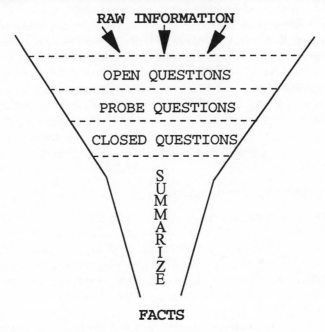

**Figure 8.3** *Information filter model*

## Presenting information

One of the most important pieces of information you need to present, right at the beginning of the interview, is the reason for, and purpose of, the interview. Without this information you could end up with two very different perceptions of what the interview was about.

A useful skill in presenting information is to be able to direct the conversation towards the desired outcome of the interview. This means only presenting information that is directly related to that outcome. One of the great traps during an interview is to allow ourselves to be taken down a side track, away from the main focus. While this may produce some very interesting information, it might not be very relevant. The skill therefore is to keep the interview 'on-course' by presenting relevant questions that take the listener from where they are now in their knowledge and understanding, to where you want them to be.

Feedback is also important in this context as you need to check that the information you have presented has been correctly interpreted and understood. It is not enough to surmise that the interviewee has understood because they are nodding or saying 'yes'. They may be too timid to say that they don't really understand.

A further skill is to recognize when to continue with, or build on, ideas that have already been introduced. If you have been able to clarify the interviewee's understanding so far then you may decide that you are able to build on some of that information. This may also enable you to elicit further information from the interviewee.

A further skill in presenting information, and one which is most often neglected, is knowing when to bring an interview to a close. In other words, to stop presenting information. Many interviews go on longer than necessary and then gradually stutter to an end because the interviewer does not have the skill to close the interview. One of the easiest ways to do this is to summarize the main points that have been covered and then ask for the interviewee's agreement to any further action that has been decided. It is then simply a matter of thanking the interviewee for their time and co-operation and saying goodbye.

## Managing the emotional content

Every interview, no matter what its purpose, has an emotional content that you will need to manage. Included here are the more obvious emotional reactions, such as anger, frustration and tears. But there will also be less obvious emotional feelings encountered during an interview. Feeling uncomfortable, frightened, tense, nervous, are all quite common, particularly when the outcome of the interview is important for the interviewee.

If you are unused to dealing with such feelings in a positive way then you can badly affect the outcome of the interview, sometimes to the extent that nothing can be salvaged from it. What can help you, as interviewer, to manage the emotional content is to attempt to understand where the feelings are coming from. Some will be brought to the interview by the interviewee and will often depend on the importance of the interview. They may also be a function of the interviewee's personality and you may be aware of this before the interview. It may be that there are traumatic events happening, that you are not aware of, in the interviewee's personal life. We refer to the emotions that are brought to an interview from 'outside' as emotional baggage.

Other emotions may be created by your ineffectual handling of the interview itself. An inexperienced interviewer, who does not yet recognize emotional undertones during a discussion, can actually exacerbate the emotion and bring it to the surface. If you then fail to handle that emotion effectively, the interview may be unsuccessful.

There are a number of ways you can manage the emotional content of an interview to ensure that it reaches the desired outcome.

1.  Being aware of the possibility of emotive issues being discussed is the first step. Recognizing that the interviewee will bring other emotional baggage to the interview, feelings about you, the organization, themselves, and, at least in the early stages of the interview, this may influence how they respond to you.
2.  Recognizing that you will be bringing emotional baggage into the interview. Feelings about the organization, the task, the job and your ability to handle the interview. These too will affect the progress of the interview and how you respond to the interviewee. Try to leave these feelings at the door. Just as you can pick up negative feelings from the interviewee, they can pick them up from you.
3.  Tied into these considerations is the environment in which the interview is to take place. As with the learning environment, how it is set up and managed will send certain messages to the interviewee. Sitting across the desk from the interviewee can create barriers, which in turn will evoke an emotional response. Conversely, sitting too closely alongside someone can be equally threatening.
4.  Avoiding interruptions to the interview is also essential. If you are being continually disturbed, it can convey to the interviewee that what they have to say is not a priority and can induce feelings of anger and frustration. Both are counter-productive to the interview.

## ACTIVITY

Identify the types of interview you may be required to hold. Alongside each one identify the kinds of emotions that may be present and indicate possible reasons for them.

As you can see, the combination of skills required for eliciting, presenting and managing the emotional content of interviews is considerable. They are used in different combinations depending on the context and purpose of the interview. For example, in a simple fact-finding interview you may use 60 per cent eliciting skills, 20 per cent presenting skills and 20 per cent managing the emotional content. In a counselling interview, however, you may use 40 per cent eliciting skills, 20 per cent presenting skills and 40 per cent managing the emotional content. It is important, therefore, to remember the purpose of the interview and be aware of the strategy you wish to adopt. This will enable you to take better control over the interview, and, ultimately, to achieve the desired outcome.

# EFFECTIVE NEGOTIATION

Everyone needs to be able to negotiate. It is something we do from being young children. Why is it then, when we put negotiating in a work context, it can become difficult or almost impossible to do? It may be partly to do with culture, the culture that we are raised in as opposed to the organizational culture. In British culture, for example, bargaining with a provider of goods to achieve a lower price is 'just not done', yet up to 75 per cent of the world's population buy and sell goods with no fixed price.

Perhaps a more difficult barrier to overcome, however, is our perception of negotiation as a highly skilled activity. We can often find it incredibly difficult to transfer our 'non-work' negotiation skills into a work environment. But this makes the assumption that we are already skilled negotiators outside work. This section will cover in some detail a possible strategy for you to adopt whatever your current skill level.

Negotiation can be described as the process by which we attempt to satisfy our needs when someone else controls what we want. To be able to negotiate effectively you must have a positive attitude, but you also need to be very clear that there is an opportunity for negotiation in the first instance.

## ACTIVITY

Identify the opportunities you have for negotiation when carrying out your training role.

There are a range of negotiating opportunities in the average workplace and they could include the some of the following:

- numbers of participants on a programme;
- the start or finish time of a programme;
- your holiday time;
- working overtime;
- use of resources;
- secretarial or administrative support;
- to get photocopying done;
- to change a procedure;
- to change a programme;
- to develop a programme;
- to increase or widen your role;
- to swap work with a colleague;
- acquisition of resources;
- personal development;
- during appraisal;

- developing and assessing learners;
- presenting a design brief to clients.

To be a successful negotiator you need to be able to identify opportunities for negotiation, and to have a positive attitude towards conflict. Conflict is a normal part of working life and can be extremely constructive. Your attitude influences your objective and these objectives in turn control how we negotiate. How we negotiate largely determines the outcome of that negotiation. You need to develop a win/win philosophy.

A win/win philosophy is essential to negotiating because each party in the negotiation wants to win. If you go into a negotiation with the view that you don't care what the other person wants, that you are going to win regardless, then your negotiation, along with any future relationship, is in jeopardy. Win/win is possible because we all have reasons for entering into negotiations with each other. They may not be the same reasons, but this is not important. What is important is both parties leaving the negotiation feeling they have achieved a large part of what they set out for without conceding everything.

In successful negotiation, the negotiator will obtain something of greater value in exchange for something they value relatively lower. You may have wanted more but will be satisfied with a large part of what you wanted. To be successful at win/win negotiating you need to:

- have a positive attitude;
- be co-operative;
- be flexible and willing to make concessions;
- be genuinely interested in the needs of the other person;
- have a high tolerance of conflict;
- be able to compromise;
- be patient;
- be able to listen to what the other person is really saying;
- have researched the issues fully;
- be able to tolerate stress.

This is quite a daunting list of characteristics and skills, and not everyone possesses them. You can develop them, at least in the context of negotiation, with practice.

## ACTIVITY

Using the list of skills and characteristics identified above, assess your personal strength against each one. Rate yourself out of 10; 1 being low, 10 being high. Having done this, list the areas you feel you would like to develop and how you can do this.

Thorough preparation is the key to successful negotiation. If you prepare thoroughly for the negotiation you are less likely to be surprised into an emotional reaction. Developing a preparation strategy that helps you will facilitate the negotiation process. Use the following questions to help you prepare for any negotiation, major or minor. It will not take as long for a minor negotiation but you need to be just as thorough.

## 1. Defining goals and objectives
- What do I want from the negotiation?
- What am I prepared to give up to get what I want?
- What is the minimum I require to meet my needs?
- Are there any time or financial constraints involved?

## 2. Major issues
- What are the issues around this negotiation for me?
- How strong is my position?
- How can I present this position to the other person?
- What are the possible issues for the other person?
- How strong is their position?
- How might they present their position?
- Are there any significant gaps between the two positions?
- Is there any common ground within the two positions?

## 3. Information gathering
- What do I know about the person I will be negotiating with?
- Where and when will the negotiation take place?
- Does this have advantages or disadvantages for me?
- Does this have advantages or disadvantages for the other person?
- Is there any personal power that I have that can be used positively in the negotiation?

## 4. Creating the right atmosphere
- How can I establish a win/win atmosphere?
- How can I begin to establish a rapport with the other person?
- What emotions might surface during the negotiation?
- How can I counter them?

## 5. Identifying and coping with conflict
- What are the major points of conflict likely to be?
- How can I differentiate between what the other person wants and what they need?
- What am I prepared to concede during the negotiation?
- What do I expect to get from the other person in return for any concessions I make?
- What is my attitude to conflict?
- What is the other person's attitude to conflict likely to be?

### 6. Finalizing the negotiation

- Does the outcome need to be recorded in any way?
- Is it dependent on approval from elsewhere? If so, how long will it take?
- Who else needs to know the outcome?
- What needs to be done to implement the outcome?

Effective negotiation is a skill that can only be learned with practice, but, once learned, is a powerful tool for any trainer, particularly as you work towards extending your influence within your organization.

## GATHERING INFORMATION

As you begin to develop your influence within your training and development role, your need for effective information gathering will increase. Effective information gathering is vital, whether it is for an organizational training needs analysis, identifying a performance problem or negotiating a training intervention. Incomplete or incorrect information can have serious consequences both for your credibility and that of your department.

There are a number of methods you can use and the one(s) you choose will depend on the resources you have at your disposal. Interviewing, for example, is quite a costly way to gather information but in some contexts, for example, skills analysis, it is often the most effective.

There are two kinds of information you can collect: quantitative and qualitative. Quantitative information is concerned with 'how many', 'how much', 'how long'. It is normally expressed in numbers or percentages. For example, 60 per cent of the complaints are attributable to the service department.

Qualitative information is generally concerned with attitudes, beliefs, values, feelings, etc. It is often more difficult to collect than quantitative information but can tell you more about a situation than quantitative can.

The kind of method you use will depend on the reason for collecting information and the kind of data you require. Methods include:

- interviewing
- questionnaires
- literature search
- observation
- analysing records
- attitude surveys
- group discussion

You will probably find that you will use more than one method to gather information, as you can get a broader picture in this way.

Attitude surveys, questionnaires and analysing records will usually give you quantitative information. Interviewing, observation and group discussion will give you qualitative information.

You probably already use a questionnaire or attitude survey to help you evaluate training programmes. Analysing records and observation can help you identify possible performance problems. Interviewing and group discussion can be useful in identifying barriers to change.

It is beyond the scope of this chapter to cover each of the methods in depth as each is complex in its own right. Many useful texts exist that can further help you develop your knowledge in this area and they are identified at the end of the chapter.

## CONSULTING AND ADVISING

So far, this chapter has been concerned with the generic or cross-functional skills needed by effective trainers. The skills identified are also central to a consultancy or advisory role, however, whether that takes place within your organization or for your organization within another. The resulting personal development should have prepared you well for taking a more active part in the decision-making and influencing process characterized by consultancy. Consultancy is working with an organization to produce significant and long-term organizational development and, therefore, change.

There are a number of major differences between training and consultancy and they occur at a number of levels. There are also several transferable skills, ie, skills that are common to both. We can begin to identify similarities and differences by comparing the training cycle with the consulting cycle.

The training cycle was considered in detail in chapter 2 (p. 31) and consists of identifying the need, designing the intervention, delivering the intervention, and then evaluating its effectiveness.

The consulting cycle generally consists of the following stages:

1. Gain entry.
2. Agree a working contract.
3. Information gathering, analysis and diagnosis.
4. Formulate proposals.
5. Feedback to clients and gain decision to implement.
6. Implementation.
7. Feedback and follow-up.

Both models are cycles in that information generated by the last stage may require a return to an earlier stage. A major difference, however, is that the training cycle consists of easily defined and separate stages that rarely overlap, whereas the consulting cycle's stages often overlap significantly. There is much more ambiguity in consultancy work than in the more straightforward training.

Skills that can be transferred from training to consulting include:

• knowledge of organizations;
• presentation skills;
• interpersonal skills;
• interviewing and counselling skills;
• observation and analysis;

- diagnosis of training needs;
- knowledge of various training design models;
- designing interventions or solutions;
- planning and organizing resources;
- budgeting;
- group and individual process skills;
- coaching and feedback skills.

Effective consultation requires collaboration. You need to negotiate your working relationship with each individual customer sponsoring a consultancy project.

As an internal consultant you are likely to encounter some resistance to such a collaborative approach, especially if you are viewed as 'the trainer'. Being the trainer can have certain connotations for the client-consultant relationship. As an external consultant you may experience different barriers, depending on the culture of the organization and the task you have been set. See the Activity box.

---

## ACTIVITY

Identify factors that could affect the relationship between the consultant and the customer. Consider this from both an internal and external perspective.

---

The following are some common examples you will probably have listed for the Activity exercise:

- the culture of the organization;
- a previous relationship (trainer and course member, or boss and subordinate);
- difference in status between the consultant and the manager;
- manager's preconceptions about trainers or consultants;
- your preconceptions about managers;
- feeling pressure to prove yourself or justify your existence;
- the manager wanting to abdicate responsibility for the problem to the consultant;
- the consultant just being used as a temporary 'extra pair of hands';
- being pressured to take on a consultancy project by your own manager;
- client manager being pressured into using a consultant by their manager;
- consultant's fear of being used as a scapegoat or of making the situation worse.

These can all be genuine issues or concerns and there are a number of steps you can take and skills you can use, as a budding consultant, to lessen their impact.

1. Be self-confident: having a strong base of self-esteem built on the foundations of your skill as a trainer and developer can help counteract any negative client perceptions of your role and ability, without your having to resort to defensive measures to justify your involvement.
2. Listen to your clients: do not do all the talking in your endeavour to impress. Clients want to feel that you understand their problems and concerns. Remember your meetings skills!
3. Resist the temptation to be rushed into agreeing a contract: the contract may be a formal, written one or simply a verbal agreement between you and the client as to the aims and objectives of your intervention. Being assertive with the client will help you avoid being pressured into a hasty response to the situation.
4. Negotiate what is on offer: be willing to talk about what you can and cannot do as a consultant. Being Superman or Superwoman and allowing unrealistic expectations in your client can produce disastrous consequences. As with any negotiating situation be prepared to say what you need from your client to ensure success and what you would like in order to be able to work at your best.
5. Recognize feelings of discomfort: they are signs that issues are not being addressed or acknowledged. In your desire to get down to work it is easy to dismiss or ignore feelings you have that are telling you 'all is not right'. Ignoring them can put you in a difficult position later, particularly where a scapegoat is required, or the client wants to abdicate all responsibility for the problem. It is important that you find ways to raise these issues with the client.
6. Ask direct questions: in any situation that requires change, some vulnerability will be felt by the client. Avoiding issues can lead to compromise and collusion with the client in order to minimize or avoid this vulnerability. Asking direct or awkward questions, and making sure the client answers them, and not some interpretation of the original question, will result in a constructive challenging of the situation.

As you can see, being a training consultant within or for an organization is quite different from being a trainer. It requires specific skills and knowledge if you are to be effective. These include:

- being able to gain entry;
- agreeing working contracts;
- gathering data;
- diagnosing issues;
- creative design of interventions;
- tolerance of ambiguity;
- achieving and maintaining a long term view;
- maintaining a broader perspective;
- understanding the nature of change;
- being able to handle conflict;

- building relationships;
- facilitating change;
- knowing the limits of your own competence;
- active listening;
- negotiating;
- presenting information;
- knowledge of the organization's operating environment;
- team working.

## ACTIVITY

On the basis of the information given in this section, identify the opportunities you have for providing consultation and advice.

## SUMMARY

This chapter has covered a range of knowledge required to underpin your development as a trainer and consultant and you should now be developing your consultancy and advisory skills in the workplace.

You were encouraged to identify opportunities for working informally within your organization and this led on to look at how you could make presentations more effectively in order to influence others. You also looked at how you could do this in the way that you contributed to meetings.

You then looked at how you could influence more effectively in writing by producing well-written and well-presented reports. It was at this point that you were asked to examine issues of access to, and confidentiality of, records. Interviewing skills came next, and you were able to identify the range of techniques embedded in interviewing. You also looked at the ratio of those skills in relation to the purpose of the interview. This was followed by effective negotiation skills and you were able to identify common problems and possible strategies to overcome them.

Effective information gathering is one of the key components of consulting and advising and in this section you were given a brief overview of some of the methods at your disposal. Finally, you were able to identify the opportunities you have within your role for providing consultancy and advice within your organization.

All the skills referred to in this chapter are essential to the trainer who wishes to develop his/her role further than simply designing and delivering training. They will enable you to become a well-rounded human resource development professional, and will increase the credibility and influence of the training function within your organization.

# Further useful reading

Allender, S (1991) *Report Writing*, BACIE, London.

Becker, P (1993) *Powerful Presentation Skills*, Addison Wesley, Massachusetts.

Bell, A H (1990) *Mastering the Meeting Maze*, Addison Wesley, Massachusetts.

Ehrenborg, J and Mattock, J (1993) *Powerful Presentations. 50 Original Ideas for Making a Real Impact*, Kogan Page, London.

Fletcher, J (1995) *Conducting Effective Interviews*, Kogan Page, London.

Gill, J and Johnson, P (1991) *Research Methods for Managers*, Paul Chapman Publishing, London.

Haynes, M E (1988) *Effective Meeting Skills*, Kogan Page, London.

Maddux, R B (1988) *Successful Negotiation*, Kogan Page, London.

Manchester Open Learning (1993) *Handling Conflict and Negotiation*, Kogan Page, London.

Manchester Open Learning (1993) *Making Effective Presentations*, Kogan Page, London.

Mandel, S (1993) *Effective Presentation Skills*, revised edition, Kogan Page, London.

Owen, M (1991) *Productive Presentations*, BACIE, London.

Peel, M (1988) *How to Make Meetings Work*, Kogan Page, London.

Phillips, K and Shaw, P (1989) *A Consultancy Approach for Trainers*, Gower, Aldershot.

Robinson, C (1995) *Effective Negotiation*, Kogan Page, London.

Saunders, M and Holdaway, K (1992) *The In-house Trainer as Consultant*, Kogan Page, London.

Stevens, M (1987) *Improving Your Presentation Skills. A Complete Action Kit*, Kogan Page, London.

Vicar, R (1994) *How to Speak and Write Persuasively*, Kogan Page, London.

Walmsley, H (1994) *Counselling Techniques for Managers*, Kogan Page, London.

# 9

## Quality through evaluation

### INTRODUCTION

In chapter 2 (p. 31) we discussed the training cycle, and evaluation was briefly described. Many trainers and managers see the training cycle as a stage process and regard evaluation as the final stage in that process. After the need has been identified, the design brief carried out, and the intervention delivered, the effect of the intervention should be evaluated. This is unfortunate, as we shall see, since it does not reflect the cyclical nature of training and development. Also, by regarding evaluation as something that 'happens at the end' much of the potential benefit that evaluation can offer, both to individuals and the organization, is lost. The process of evaluation, however, is the one most likely to be either ignored, or paid lip service to. Whether you are a trainer, on your own or as part of a department, a manager or a consultant, you ignore evaluation at your peril.

This chapter explores the issues of quality and evaluation when applied to training and development. It begins by identifying why organizations need to evaluate training interventions. This includes achieving a quality product and therefore developing a quality workforce. It explores the different kinds of evaluation strategies, levels and stages available to the evaluator and the benefits that can be obtained from each one.

Evaluation is of little benefit, however, if the results of the evaluation are not then used. The results allow us to see how the outcomes of the evaluation can be fed back into the training cycle to improve the process for any future interventions. They can also help us to incorporate any innovations in training and development by identifying whether or not they are appropriate for the organization's training and development plan.

### DEFINING EVALUATION

There are three measures that we can apply to a training programme or intervention: internal validation, external validation, and evaluation. Sometimes the term validation is used synonymously with evaluation but it is only part of the evaluation process.

The Manpower Services Commission *Glossary of Training Terms* (1981) describes these terms as follows:

*Internal validation: A series of tests and assessments designed to ascertain whether a training programme has achieved the behavioural objectives specified.*

*External validation: A series of tests and assessments designed to ascertain whether the behavioural objectives of an internally valid training programme were realistically based on an accurate initial identification of training needs in relation to the criteria of effectiveness adopted by the organization.*

*Evaluation: The assessment of the total value of a training system, training course or programme in social as well as financial terms. Evaluation differs from validation in that it attempts to measure the overall cost benefit of the course or programme and not just the achievement of its laid down objectives. The term is also used in the general judgmental sense of the continuous monitoring of a programme or of the training function as a whole.*

But to what extent are these definitions and distinctions useful to us in practice?

## Internal validation

Internal validation is useful to us because the focus of attention is on whether or not the performance objectives specified for the intervention have been achieved. This can be applied to a unit of learning or a whole programme, depending on what outcomes were regarded as essential to the success of the intervention. The results of internal validation are then used to improve the quality of future interventions and are therefore of benefit to both future deliverers and learners. So internal validation provides us with a basic quality control mechanism for training and development. In chapter 5 (p. 94) some possible measures of internal validation were given under the headings of subjective and objective testing. Other measures are discussed later in this chapter.

## External validation

The issue here is whether or not the participants in the intervention, having achieved the outcomes identified in the design brief, can successfully apply their new skills in their job. Has learning transfer taken place? The major issues affecting learning transfer were discussed in chapter 5 (p. 96) and include accurate identification of the performance problem and therefore of the training need, the design of an appropriate intervention, and its effective delivery; in other words, the other three processes which are embedded in the experiential training cycle.

External validation is concerned, therefore, with the wider application of the performance objectives identified and assessed during the internal validation process, and both internal and external validation requirements should be an integral consideration when designing a training intervention. Ways of measuring this validity are discussed later in this chapter.

## Evaluation

Evaluation uses the tools of internal and external validation to provide a wider-reaching analysis of the effectiveness of a training intervention or programme. It is also concerned with the costs and benefits of carrying out the intervention and its impact on the organization in a much broader sense than simply the effective application of new skills. For example:

A medium-sized manufacturing company wished to develop its supervisors as team leaders in order to improve the effectiveness of both the supervisors and their staff. They had decided to do this as they felt that creating a team philosophy within the organization would lead to many benefits for both the individuals and the organization. Without an evaluation process, however, it would be almost impossible to attribute any changes evidenced as a result of this intervention. By building into the design brief a series of measures such as post-course evaluation questionnaires, action plans, debriefing sessions with their managers, and the monitoring of quantitative data on such diverse measures as absenteeism, reject rates and output, the organization was able to identify a number of improvements directly attributable to the intervention.

## WHY EVALUATE?

As we have said, many training programmes or interventions are not evaluated and later in this chapter we shall look at why this may be so. Before we do this, however, we need to identify the benefits that can be gained by carrying out the evaluation (see the Activity box overleaf).

There are a whole range of benefits to be obtained from the validation and evaluation of training and development activities and all can be used to justify what is often seen to be an unnecessary and time-consuming procedure. They include identifying whether:

- performance objectives were met;
- participants were satisfied with the process;
- customers' needs were met;
- change in performance can be measured;
- change in performance is due to the training intervention;

**ACTIVITY**

Earlier in this chapter we referred briefly to some of the benefits of validation and evaluation. With these as a starting point identify the benefits to be gained by your organization as a result of carrying out validation and evaluation of its training and development activities. This should also include any external provision, either as a deliverer or as a customer.

- learning transfer has taken place;
- the training is contributing to a more effective organization;
- the training function is performing effectively, ie providing a quality service;
- external providers are giving value for money;
- any modifications need to be made to future programmes.

These benefits can be classified as follows:

1. The quality of the intervention.
2. The development of the individual.
3. The performance of the organization.
4. The performance of the training function.

Of the four, the one that is so often missed is the performance of the training function. Again, this refers to all those involved in the training and development process, both internal and external to the organization. Systematic validation and evaluation of the activities of a training department or training organization can provide much needed justification when competing for funds or business.

In chapter 8 (p. 171) we looked at the different kinds of data or information that can be collected, the ways of collecting them, and identified the differences between quantitative and qualitative information. Quantitative data of the kind generated by the evaluation process can greatly strengthen your position in the market place by providing clear evidence of the achievements of the training function.

Given the benefits of evaluation, why does it so rarely happen? (See the Activity box.)

**ACTIVITY**

You have probably been a participant in and deliverer of training interventions where evaluation did not take place. What were the possible reasons for this?

The following are common reasons for the absence of an effective evaluation strategy:

The course provider:

- did not feel it was necessary;
- felt it would be too time consuming;
- thought it might cost too much;
- felt that it was not appropriate because of the subject of the intervention;
- did not have any clearly identifiable or measurable outcomes;
- could not identify any specific criteria against which the programme could be evaluated;
- could not be bothered;
- was not asked to;
- did not know how;
- felt the participants would not want to be bothered;
- felt it would be unacceptable as the participants were too senior within the organization.

Many of the above reasons are commonly used as justification for not evaluating a training intervention. Unfortunately, without effective evaluation, there are a number of potential consequences.

## Consequences of not evaluating

1. The trainer cannot effectively judge his/her own performance.
2. The training manager cannot effectively judge the performance of his or her trainers.
3. The effectiveness of the design brief cannot be assessed.
4. The reactions of the participants to the intervention cannot be identified.
5. The participants cannot measure, assess or record their own progress without clearly identified criteria and feedback.
6. Opportunities to motivate participants are lost.
7. Attributing change in performance to the intervention is almost impossible.
8. Transfer of learning cannot be assessed.
9. The customer has no way of knowing the extent of the effectiveness of the intervention.
10. The customer cannot quantify the costs and benefits of the intervention.

The next section identifies a number of models you can use to evaluate the effectiveness of a training intervention or programme.

## MODELS OF EVALUATION

There are a number of tried and tested evaluation models available 'off-the-shelf' and they include:

- Kirkpatrick's model;
- Parker's model;
- the Ciro model;
- Hamblin's model.

### Kirkpatrick's model

This model requires the collection and evaluation of data from the following four levels:

| | |
|---|---|
| Reaction: | the learner's reaction to the intervention. |
| Learning: | the learning achieved within the intervention. |
| Behaviour: | any change brought about by the intervention. |
| Results: | the positive effects of that change in behaviour on the organization. |

### Parker's model

This model also identifies four levels for data collection and evaluation.

**Participant satisfaction:**
the learner's reactions to the intervention identified by questionnaire.

**Participant knowledge gained:**
the gains evaluated by means of pre- and post-testing of skills and knowledge.

**Job performance:**
evaluated by objective measurement of job performance post-intervention.

**Group performance:**
evaluation of the results of the whole group. A much broader and more difficult evaluation.

### The Ciro model

This model gets its name from the four categories of evaluation identified, Context, Input, Reaction, Outcome (CIRO) and was developed by Warr, Bird and Rackham in 1970.

**Context evaluation**
This covers a review of the:

- current conditions relating to the operational context of the intervention.
- identification of training needs.
- ultimate objectives – the performance problem to be overcome.
- intermediate objectives – the changes in operational performance behaviour necessary to achieve the ultimate objective.
- immediate objectives – the acquisition of the knowledge, skills and attitudes leading to the intermediate objective.

**Input evaluation**
This is an assessment of the use of all the resources used in the training intervention, including an evaluation of the feasible alternatives.

**Reaction evaluation**
This refers to the systematic collection of participants' reactions to the intervention, both during and after it.

**Outcome evaluation**
This proceeds through four stages:

1. Defining the training objectives.
2. Constructing instruments for measuring the achievement of the objectives.
3. Using these instruments at appropriate times.
4. Reviewing the results and using them to improve subsequent programmes.

## Hamblin's model

This model identifies five levels of evaluation.

| | |
|---|---|
| Level 1 | Reaction: evaluation of the learner's reaction to the intervention. It includes the style, method, environment, tutor performance, etc. It is carried out during, immediately after, and some time after the event. |
| Level 2 | Learning: this is an evaluation of the development that has taken place in skills, knowledge and attitude. It can be carried out before and after the intervention. |
| Level 3 | Job behaviour: to find out if job performance has changed as a result of the intervention. It should be carried out before and after the intervention. |
| Level 4 | Department and organization: to quantify the effect on the |

learner's department or group. Cost benefit analysis can ascertain this.

Level 5    Ultimate value: to what extent the intervention has affected the ultimate profitability and/or survival of the organization. Extremely difficult to quantify as many other factors may be involved apart from training and development.

As you can see, the four models have a lot in common with each other. They all identify stages or categories of evaluation that roughly equate to each other. By identifying appropriate stages or levels within the evaluation process you can begin to devise or adapt a system to enable you to evaluate training and development interventions you are involved in.

The four levels that can be identified from the above models are:

- Level 1 – reactions.
- Level 2 – learning.
- Level 3 – job performance.
- Level 4 – department and organization.

The first thing you need to ensure, therefore, is that you have clearly identified objectives for each level of the evaluation process. This requires you to build the objectives into the design of the programme. Lack of such objectives was identified earlier in the chapter as one of the reasons why an intervention may not be evaluated. If you do not build in the mechanism – in this case clearly measurable outcomes directly related to the learner's behaviour – then it is impossible to quantify any benefit from the intervention.

## Setting objectives

### Level 1 – Reactions

What sort of reactions are you attempting to generate in the learners? This refers to the level of satisfaction with all aspects of the intervention including: environment, tutors, pace and level of delivery, relevance, methods and media used and domestic arrangements. See chapter 5 (p. 80) and chapter 7 (p. 125).

### Level 2 – Learning

These are the performance objectives or learning outcomes required as a result of the intervention. See chapter 4 (p. 62).

### Level 3 – Job performance

These objectives are concerned with the changes in the learner's job performance directly related to the performance objectives and learning outcomes required. The issue here is that of the transfer of learning to the workplace.

### Level 4 – Department and organization

These objectives can be extremely difficult to set as they are concerned with the improvements and changes at a macro level within the organization. They can include such measures as increased production, productivity and flexibility. They can also be difficult to measure as other factors may concurrently influence the outcome.

---

**ACTIVITY**

Using the training interventions that you are involved in or familiar with, identify at what levels evaluation takes place. At the same time, identify the objectives against which the evaluation is measured.

---

Now that you are familiar with the stages of evaluation we can identify the tools that can help you carry out the process.

## TOOLS OF EVALUATION

There are a number of tools available to help you carry out an evaluation of a training intervention and they are grouped here by level. It is not intended to explore these tools in detail as there are many excellent books already available on this subject. They are identified at the end of this chapter.

## Level 1

This level equates to the definition of internal validation given above. Although the information from this level can be collected through a discussion with the group, the most common method used to collect data is by reaction questionnaire. This type of questionnaire can help you obtain feedback on participants' reactions to the training intervention. It is usually administered at the end of the training intervention and could include questions on the following:

- Was attendance a result of an identified training need?
- Were the programme objectives identified and explained?
- Were the programme objectives met?
- Opportunities for group discussion.
- Opportunities for individual contribution.
- Effectiveness of the tutor or facilitator.
- Timing of the sessions.
- Course organization, including venue, food, and timing.
- Course content, including level, delivery methods and resources.

- Personal development experienced.
- Relevance to your needs.
- What could be added to the programme?
- Was anything unnecessary in the programme?
- Any other comments.

It is important that this feedback is obtained and then acted on as a failure to address these basic issues can result in participants feeling dissatisfied with the programme, and, therefore, with their development. There are a number of factors you need to consider when designing such a questionnaire.

As the questionnaire is to be completed at the end of the programme or intervention it needs to be kept as short as possible otherwise you run the risk of participants rushing through the questions without giving their responses much thought. This will affect the accuracy of the information you obtain. Decide what you need to know and keep the questions short. Use a rating scale so that you can obtain quantitative data, but make sure you have an even number of boxes or categories so that people do not just choose the middle one. For example:

| | | | | | | | | |
|---|---|---|---|---|---|---|---|---|
| How useful were the discussion groups? | | | | | | | | |
| Not useful | 1 | 2 | 3 | 4 | 5 | 6 | Very useful | |

Do not ask more than one question in the same sentence as you will not know which of the categories the answer refers to. For example:

| |
|---|
| How useful did you find the one-to-one sessions and discussion groups? |

You can also ask for a combination of qualitative and quantitative information. For example:

| | | | | | | | | |
|---|---|---|---|---|---|---|---|---|
| How useful were the discussion groups? | | | | | | | | |
| Not useful | 1 | 2 | 3 | 4 | 5 | 6 | Very useful | |
| Why was this? | | | | | | | | |

Once you have formulated your questions try them out on a couple of colleagues before you give the questionnaire to participants, to make sure that the questions are clear and unambiguous.

## Level 2

This level is also concerned with internal validation. Here you are collecting information on the development of knowledge, skills and attitudes. To enable a valid comparison to be made, however, you will need to collect this information before the intervention, in order to establish existing levels. This is not always possible, however, particularly if it is a completely new area of development for the participant. If this is the case then you simply attribute any development in knowledge, skills or attitudes to the training intervention. If the programme is developing on existing areas then you will want to quantify to what extent the knowledge, skills and attitudes shown after the event are attributable to it. There are various ways you can do this.

### Knowledge

Chapter 5 (p. 94) compares a number of objective and subjective methods suitable for the assessment of knowledge and understanding.

### Skills

Chapter 10 (p. 207) identifies a range of methods for assessing the development of skills and competence. They include:

- using pre-programme performance records;
- observation of performance during practice or simulation;
- learner self-assessment;
- performance tests during and at the end of the programme;
- assignments;
- projects.

### Attitudes

Change in attitude is much more difficult to assess than change in knowledge or skill. The following methods may help:

- interviews;
- case studies;
- role playing;
- attitude questionnaires;
- group discussions.

## Level 3

This is the level of external validation. Here you are attempting to measure any changes in job behaviour occurring as a result of the training intervention, and, therefore, learning transfer. Many of the tools identified in levels 1 and 2 can also be used in the workplace to assess performance changes. However, it may not always be possible for trainers to carry out this stage of the process.

Operational difficulties may prevent you from evaluating the effects of the intervention over a period of time and you may need to enlist the help of line managers and supervisors to do this for you. The methods identified here are suitable, therefore, for use by both trainers and non-trainers. They include:

- performance rating scales completed by the line manager;
- observation, with or without the use of checklists;
- using reports and assignments to demonstrate the application of knowledge and skills;
- comparing performance records pre- and post-training;
- formal and informal questioning;
- formal and informal interviews;
- appraisal by line manager;
- self-appraisal and reporting.

## Level 4

It is at this level that the trainer usually has least input. This can be for a number of reasons: lack of opportunity; the difficulty of collecting data at this level; the culture of the organization; the perceived lack of need; in fact for all the reasons identified at the beginning of this chapter. As level 4 is the level at which benefits to the organization can be identified, however, it is an ideal opportunity for you to claim credit for the improvements in performance. Enhancing your status as a trainer, manager or consultant will then have a knock-on effect on your department or business.

There are no specific techniques available to carry out evaluation at this level. By returning to the organizational climate indicators identified during the training needs analysis however, you should be able to assess the effectiveness of the intervention by measuring any changes in those criteria. Chapter 6 (p. 112) covers the sources of such criteria, for example:

- absenteeism;
- wastage rates (of people and materials);
- accidents;
- productivity;
- customer feedback;
- error rates;
- sales figures.

Your aim is to demonstrate that the improvements are a direct result of the training intervention. You could also take this one stage further and carry out a cost benefit analysis of the intervention in an attempt to quantify the financial benefits of training and development.

Costing training was covered in depth in chapter 7 (p. 132–5). Financially quantifying the benefits is a much more difficult process, however, especially if you are developing 'soft' performance skills such as assertiveness, report writing or counselling. It is much easier if you are developing 'hard' performance skills such as information processing, welding or machining, as the outputs can be clearly identified and measured. Identifying the effects of assertiveness training against production or service criteria can be almost impossible. Costing the benefits becomes almost impossible too. It is beyond the scope of this book to go into greater detail, but there are a number of references to cost benefit analysis at the end of this chapter if you wish to find out more.

---

### ACTIVITY

Carry out an evaluation of a training programme or intervention that you are familiar with. You should produce a report covering all four levels of the evaluation process, clearly identifying which tools you used and why. The results should indicate the benefits obtained from the intervention as well as any proposals for modifications to future interventions.

---

All the tools and techniques available to you are of little value if you do not use them in a standardized and systematic way. This is because you will not be able to compare results from different individuals or groups with any accuracy. To ensure that your evaluation processes are valid and reliable therefore you need to have a standard procedure.

## Developing procedures

If your organization is accredited to BS 5750, ISO 9000, the European Federation of Quality Management (EFQM) or has the Malcolm Baldridge National Quality Award (MBNQA) then you will already have a formal systems and procedures manual for evaluation. The following information will be useful to you if your organization does not have such a manual. It should contain:

1. Who is responsible for the various aspects of the evaluation process.
2. An index of the tools which are available.
3. The stages or times at which the tools are to be used.
4. Whom the tools were designed for, eg managers, machinists, new employees.
5. Sample or specimen tools, including tests and questionnaires.
6. Detailed procedures for administering the tools, including:
   - by whom;
   - when;

- how;
- where.

7. Guidelines on using the feedback generated by the tools, including:
   - to whom;
   - by whom;
   - how;
   - when;
   - where.
8. Procedures for recording and reviewing the feedback.
9. Procedures for designing, validating and evaluating tools.

## USING THE RESULTS

It has been highlighted throughout this chapter that evaluation in practice is often a very patchy process and usually concentrated on the first two levels, ie on internal validation. To further compound the problem it is often found that where evaluation does take place the results are not then used.

---

### ACTIVITY

Earlier in the chapter you were asked to identify at what levels evaluation of training takes place in interventions you are familiar with. Using that information as your starting point, identify what happens to the results of the evaluation.

---

Unless the results are fed back to the appropriate people, and then acted on, the evaluation may as well not have taken place. Interested parties could include:

- trainers
- managers
- training providers
- participants
- resource providers
- the venue

- consultants
- caterers
- equipment suppliers
- senior managers and/or directors

By analysing the results of the tests, questionnaires and other tools used during the evaluation process you should be able to draw conclusions about the effectiveness of the training interventions you are involved in. The results will either validate your training programme or intervention, or identify areas for improvement. The function of evaluation therefore is to systematically assess the effectiveness of a training intervention and to use the results of that assessment to inform future interventions. The ways in which it can do this are illustrated in Figure 9.1.

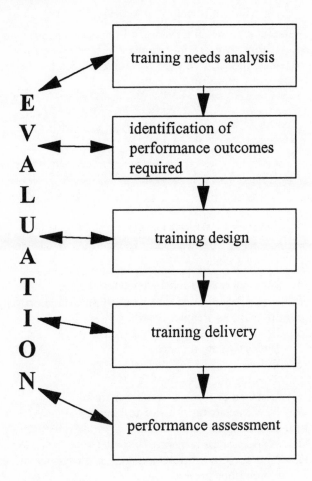

**Figure 9.1** *Effective evaluation*

Evaluation within the field of training and development is not just confined to existing training practices and interventions. In order to remain effective we need to ensure that our knowledge of theories, practices and resources is kept up to date. It is not sufficient just to be aware of these developments. We also need to evaluate their potential against the training needs of the organization.

## INCORPORATING INNOVATIONS

We saw in chapter 2 (p. 22) that training and development does not occur in a vacuum. The culture and structure of the organization has an impact on what can be achieved. As a result of this the changing needs of the organization can have an impact on the kinds of interventions you are involved in, the methods and technology of delivery, and also the criteria that are used to measure effective performance.

Rapid advances in training and development practice are taking place and, before they are incorporated into the organization's portfolio of strategies, they too need to be evaluated. See the Activity box.

---

**ACTIVITY**

Identify recent and current advances in training and development that are relevant to your organization's needs.

---

The following list is not exhaustive as different kinds of organizations and occupational sectors will be subject to their own requirements and they can be very specific.

1. National occupational standards.
2. Competence-based development and assessment.
3. Investors in People Award.
4. BS 5750 or ISO 9000.
5. Interactive multimedia.
6. Videos.
7. Training packages.
8. Distance or flexible learning materials.
9. New assessment tools or techniques.
10. Psychological tests.
11. Workplace assessment.
12. New theories of development, eg ownership and empowerment.
13. Continuous professional development.
14. Using portfolios.
15. Workplace development, eg coaching and mentoring, action planning and learning contracts.

All these developments require evaluation before a decision is made about their implementation, but unfortunately this does not always happen. At an organizational level, innovations and advances are often seized on as a means of improving performance, productivity or the public profile of the organization, without an objective assessment of the potential costs and benefits to the organization. The implications for you as a trainer and developer are therefore wide-ranging and you need to use your skills and knowledge of evaluation to influence the decision-makers about the appropriateness of any changes in practice.

Evaluation of advances at the level of training and development practice is also important, particularly where additional costs are involved. Training and development practice is a dynamic field, and, as such, advances in theory, practice and technology are now much more common than in the past.

It is important not to change just for the sake of it however. Consider all the evidence, whether it is from published reports, papers in journals, personal experience or observation in practice, consultations with colleagues or conferences and exhibitions. Only when you have considered the evidence available to you and compared it with existing practice and desired outcomes should you make your decision. In this way you can provide a reasoned justification for the change, while at the same time providing clear criteria against which you can evaluate the impact of the change during and after its implementation.

The following case study of a management development programme illustrates how this can work in practice.

The management skills programme is part of a wider management development programme for middle managers. The programme is part-time and takes two years to complete. A number of concerns had been raised by the participants about the relevance of the management skills part of the programme to their work and of their ensuing failure to transfer learning to their workplace. As a result of this it was felt necessary to change the programme to make it more effective. By clearly identifying the desired outcomes of the programme it was possible to draw up a list of criteria against which possible innovations could be measured. The criteria were:

- relevance to the work role;
- the ability to apply the model;
- evidence requirements;
- effectiveness as a management development method;
- effectiveness as a learning tool.

A number of options were evaluated against these criteria and a decision was made to use the MCI Personal Competence model. This was duly implemented and after two years of operation has now been formally evaluated against the original criteria for its selection. The results of the evaluation show that the model has been successful when measured against all the identified criteria.

As you can see, by evaluating any proposed changes before deciding to proceed you will develop a clear rationale for change. The results of the change can then be evaluated against those criteria.

## SUMMARY

The chapter began by separating out and then defining the component parts of the evaluation process, namely, internal validation, external validation and evaluation. These definitions were then placed in a practical context and the question asked 'Why evaluate?' The benefits of evaluating training and development activities were then identified.

Common reasons for not evaluating were discussed along with the potential consequences for the trainer, the participants and the organization of not evaluating.

A number of existing models of evaluation were then outlined. They included Kirkpatrick's model, Parker's model, the Ciro model and Hamblin's model and a number of levels common to each were identified. The levels were: reaction; learning; job behaviour; department or organization. Methods for assessing the effectiveness of the intervention appropriate to each stage were then identified along with a guide to the timing of the assessment.

A major outcome of evaluation – change – was then identified in the context of using the results of an evaluation. The importance of making known the results of an evaluation was stressed as this enables any lessons learned to be fed back to inform current training practice. This was complemented by the section on incorporating innovations in training and development practice.

As a trainer, manager or consultant you cannot ignore evaluation if you are to provide an effective service to the organization. By quantifying the benefits accrued as a result of the training intervention you are justifying your involvement, and protecting your future.

## References

Hamblin, A C (1974) *Evaluation and Control of Training*, McGraw Hill, London.

Kirkpatrick, D L (1976) 'Evaluation of training' in Craig, R L (ed.) *Training and Development Handbook*, McGraw Hill, London.

Manpower Services Commission (1981) *Glossary of Training Terms*, MSC, HMSO, London.

Parker, T C (1973) 'Evaluation, the forgotten finale of training', Personnel.

Warr, P, Bird M and Rackham, N (1979) *Evaluation of Management Training*, sixth edition, Gower, Aldershot.

## Further useful reading

Bramley, P (1990) *Evaluating Training Effectiveness: Translating Theory into Practice*, McGraw Hill, London.

Bramley, P (1990) *Evaluation of Training: A Practical Guide*, BACIE, London.

Calder, J (1994) *Programme Evaluation and Quality: A Comprehensive Guide to Setting up an Evaluation System*, Kogan Page, London.

Easterby Smith, M (1994) *Evaluating Management Development, Training and Development*, Gower, Aldershot.

Fletcher, S (1993) *Quality and Competence*, Kogan Page, London.

Jackson, T (1989) *Evaluation. Relating Training to Performance*, Kogan Page, London.

Mager, R (1991) *Measuring Instructional Results*, second edition, Kogan Page, London.

Newby, T (1992) *Cost-effective Training*, Kogan Page, London.

Newby, T (1992) *Validating your Training*, Kogan Page, London.

Pepper, A D (1987) *Managing the Training and Development Function*, Gower, Aldershot. (Chapter 11 discusses how to quantify the costs and benefits of training. Chapter 12, 'Cost benefit analysis', identifies the procedure and provides a number of illustrative case studies.)

Peterson, R (1992) *Training Needs Analysis in the Workplace*, Kogan Page, London.

Philips, J (1991) *Handbook of Training Evaluation and Measurement Methods*, second edition, Kogan Page, London.

Rae, L (1991) *How to Measure Training Effectiveness*, second edition, Gower, Aldershot.

Reeves, M (1993) *Evaluation of Training*, The Industrial Society, London.

Sheal, P (1994) *How to Develop and Present Staff Training Courses*, second edition, Kogan Page, London.

# 10

# Assessment and verification

## INTRODUCTION

Assessment is traditionally associated with courses. You attend a course of learning and then have to prove to the tutor or the examining body that you have learned whatever it is that is required of you. Assessment is also an integral part of other forms of training and development, however. Without the assessment of performance, either before, during or after a training intervention most of what we do as trainers would be meaningless.

Assessment practices have already been referred to extensively throughout this book, particularly in chapters 5 (p. 94) and 9 (p. 187). However, all the references to assessment so far have focused on the application of a range of methods in a general context. The focus of this chapter is on a particular kind of assessment; competence-based assessment.

With the growing number of national occupational standards available, along with NVQs and SVQs, today's trainers are increasingly being asked to assess competence-based performance. So how does it differ from traditional assessment? The emphasis in competence-based assessment is on obtaining sufficient evidence to determine whether an individual is performing competently in their job. It is concerned with the outcome of learning as reflected in an individual's performance, rather than with the learning itself.

This form of assessment is not confined to the assessment of national occupational standards, however. Many organizations have developed their own standards of performance based on workplace competence, and many of the issues identified in this chapter will be equally relevant to trainers and assessors in those organizations.

## ASSESSOR AND VERIFIER ROLES

The two roles to be explored are those of first and second line assessor. Much of the information that follows is common to both roles although, for the purpose of clarity, the role of the second line assessor is discussed in more detail towards the end of this chapter.

Some awarding bodies refer to first line assessors as workplace assessors and many combine the role of second line assessor with that of the internal verifier. If your organization is accredited to assess NVQs or SVQs it is usually known as an assessment centre for the awarding body. As an assessment centre you are required to follow the assessment processes and procedures identified by the awarding body. Each awarding body broadly follows the quality assurance model illustrated in Figure 10.1.

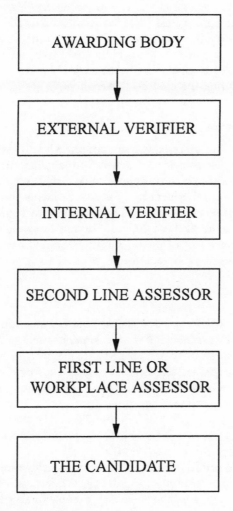

**Figure 10.1** *Competence-based assessment quality assurance process*

## The candidate

Candidates make self-assessments of their abilities judged against the occupational standards they wish to attain. They identify when they feel they are ready to be assessed and they draw up assessment plans with the first line assessor. They then present evidence of their performance, including knowledge and understanding, to the assessor.

## Workplace or first line assessor

The first line assessor works closely with the candidate and is concerned primarily with the direct assessment of the candidate's performance in the workplace through observation and questioning. By working closely with the candidate you collect and record evidence of his or her performance, make judgements against the specified standards about the competence of that performance and provide feedback to the candidate. As first line assessor it is your responsibility to make recommendations for certification of competence. It is also likely that training needs will be identified during the course of assessment.

## Second line assessor

As a second line assessor you are concerned with assessing competence using more diverse evidence drawn from a wider range of sources than the first line assessor. Such sources could include reports from supervisors or peers, historical evidence of past achievements and judgements made by other assessors. You may be working with a number of first line assessors and are likely to be more distant from the candidate, perhaps from a different part of the organization. Second line assessors may even be from an external organization.

## Internal verifier

The internal verifier is employed by your organization and is responsible for the quality assurance of the assessment system within it. This person has the responsibility of ensuring that there is consistency in the assessment decisions across all assessors. The responsibility therefore is for quality control and the internal verifier samples assessments and countersigns assessment decisions.

## External verifier

The external verifier is responsible for the quality assurance system from outside your organization. External verifiers are appointed by the awarding body for the relevant occupational standards and visit organizations on a regular basis. They liaise with an organization's internal verifiers and may sample the work of first and second line assessors. A major responsibility is to monitor and advise on the overall assessment process within an organization. They also make recommendations and provide feedback to the awarding body.

## Awarding body

The awarding body awards certificates for specified NVQs or SVQs. While each awarding body follows a similar assessment process they can determine their own assessment system. The assessment system refers to the particular recording and reporting systems required from the organization and its assessors. They have overall control of the assessment system through their relationship with the external verifiers. Your organization may be involved with more than one awarding body each with different administration systems.

---

### ACTIVITY

By finding out the answers to the following questions you will become more familiar with the quality assurance model operating within your assessment centre.

- What awarding bodies does your organization use for assessing competence?
- Who is/are the external verifier(s)?
- Who is/are the internal verifier(s)?
- Does the system require second line assessors?
- Who are the second line assessors?
- Who are the first line or workplace assessors?
- Who is responsible for co-ordinating the administration required by the awarding body?

---

## THE ASSESSMENT PROCESS

The assessment process may vary slightly between awarding bodies but there are a number of common features. Your first task should be to negotiate an assessment plan with your candidate. You will also need to decide:

- who is to be assessed and when;
- what is to be assessed and to what standards;
- what evidence is required;
- how the evidence is to be collected;
- how you are going to judge the evidence against the required standards;
- whether the candidate is 'competent', 'not yet competent', or, 'there is insufficient evidence to make a decision';
- how to record the assessment;
- how to provide feedback to the candidate on his/her performance.

This is illustrated in Figure 10.2.

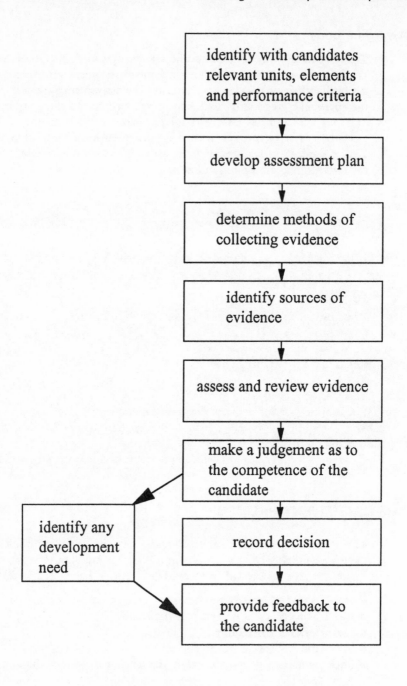

**Figure 10.2** *The assessment process*

## The assessment plan

There are a number of questions that you need to ask when meeting the candidate for the first time. This meeting is of vital importance as it allows you to clarify and plan the assessment process with the candidate. This enables you to begin your assessment relationship with the candidate in an atmosphere of shared understanding of what is to come.

---

### ACTIVITY

List the areas you consider need clarification and planning with the candidate at the start of the assessment.

---

In doing the Activity exercise, you may have included the following items:

1. Why does the candidate want to be assessed?
2. Does the candidate understand the system?
3. Which units can the candidate realistically achieve?
4. What methods of assessment are likely to be appropriate?
5. When is the assessment to take place?
6. When is the assessment plan to be reviewed?

We shall now consider these questions individually.

### Why does the candidate want to be assessed?

The answer to this question will enable you to decide, with the candidate, which qualification or award to pursue. It will also help you to find out what is motivating the candidate.

### Does the candidate understand the system?

A competence-based development and assessment system can seem very complex to someone who is used to traditional methods. By ensuring the candidate understands how standards are structured, defined and assessed you will make the assessment process much more manageable for you both.

### Which units can the candidate realistically achieve?

Answering this question can take some time as you will need to take into account evidence the candidate can provide about prior achievements, current work role and development opportunities. Also, the continuous nature of the assessment process means that these units may change as a result of evidence produced and changes in work role. What is important is that the expectations of the candidate and assessor are realistic. Unrealistic expectations will only lead to disappointment, reduced motivation or even failure to achieve.

## What methods of assessment are likely to be appropriate?

Discussion with the candidate will allow you to explore the possibilities available to you. The observation of natural work performance must be the main or primary source of evidence but there are many other kinds of assessment available to support this.

## When is the assessment to take place?

Candidate and assessor need to plan the timing of the assessment in order to take advantage of naturally occurring evidence. Also, if you are not the candidate's line manager then he/she will also need to be informed that an assessment is taking place.

## When is the assessment plan to be reviewed?

This is an often neglected component of an assessment plan. Without a clearly stated review date it is possible for assessment to 'slip'. This slows down the process and can de-motivate the candidate. By building in regular reviews you ensure that any changes identified as a result of the assessment process are acted on in a timely manner.

## COLLECTING AND ASSESSING EVIDENCE

The collection and assessment of evidence requires the assessor to be objective about both the evidence and the candidate. There are a number of issues that you need to have knowledge of, however, in order to help you develop and maintain that objectivity. They are:

- rules of evidence;
- rules of assessment methods;
- factors influencing assessment.

### Rules of evidence

The rules of evidence are concerned with the quality of evidence. There are four rules and they state that the evidence must be:

- valid;
- authentic;
- current;
- sufficient.

### Validity

The key question that you need to ask as an assessor is: 'What does this piece of evidence tell me?' The issue of validity is critical and you must be certain that the piece of evidence proves to you that the candidate can perform to the specified standards. The evidence must therefore tell you about the candidate's performance. If it does not tell you about actual performance then it is not valid.

For example, if you were assessing supervisors then you might receive documentation relating to meetings held. What does the documentation tell you? Does it tell you about the part the supervisor played in the meeting? Does it tell you how or if the supervisor made decisions, communicated information or handled conflict? It may only give a minuted account of the meeting, and the notes may have been written by a secretary. The documentation may have a role to play as supplementary or supporting evidence (discussed later in the chapter) but is not valid as performance evidence on its own.

## Authenticity

Did the candidate produce the evidence? How do you know this? You must ensure that the evidence presented relates to the candidate's own work. This is particularly important when assessing documentary evidence. You must have no doubt that the evidence was produced solely by the candidate, without the assistance of others. Using the example of the supervisor, were the minutes written by him/her? Did she/he produce the agenda?

## Currency

Evidence is only current if the information it provides the assessor with matches that specified by the standards being used. It must prove, therefore, that the candidate is currently competent, not that they were competent in the past. This is particularly important for second line assessors as historical evidence may be provided to support the current claim of competence. Factors such as changing legislation and new technology can render evidence out of date.

## Sufficiency

For the purposes of competence-based assessment *all* specified standards must be assessed. Once you have addressed the issues of validity, authenticity and currency therefore, you need to ensure that you have sufficient evidence to make a confident judgement about competence. It can often be a difficult decision for an assessor to make as you have to ensure that the evidence is of good quality and covers all the performance requirements identified within the element, its performance criteria and the range statements.

---

### ACTIVITY

The rules of evidence are essential to the competence-based assessment system. How do they actually operate in your assessment centre?

---

Newly trained assessors are often tempted to err on the side of caution. However, just as making a judgement of competence based on insufficient evidence can result in a lack of credibility, asking for more evidence than is required can result in discrimination against the candidate.

In order to apply the rules of evidence you will need to ensure the following:

1. All the specified standards are assessed.
2. The evidence clearly and directly relates to the specified standards.
3. There is sufficient evidence to cover the range specified within the standards.
4. You do not compare the performance of one candidate against another.
5. Valid assessment methods are used to generate evidence in realistic conditions.
6. Effective records are kept that enable evidence to be traced to its source.
7. The assessment process does not discriminate against the candidate by putting undue pressure on him/her.

## Rules of assessment methods

Just as there are rules to ensure the quality of evidence, there are also rules to ensure the quality of assessment methods. These rules or conditions are:

- transparency;
- validity;
- reliability.

### Transparency

Transparent means open and clear. A competence-based assessment system therefore should be open and clear to all those involved. This requires the performance standards to be accessible, easily understood and have real meaning to the people using them. It also requires the evidence criteria to be explicit so that all parties in the assessment process are clear about what is required. If the candidate's assessment plan is clear and the methods chosen for assessment are well thought out, then the roles and responsibilities for assessment are also clear.

### Validity

This follows on from transparency. A well-planned assessment is one in which the candidate and the assessor are clear on what is being assessed and what evidence will be generated. In addition to this it is necessary that the types of evidence generated, and their format, will provide realistic proof of performance to the specified standards. As an assessor you will need to ask yourself what evidence you require about the candidate's performance in order to infer competence. Then ask yourself if the assessment methods you have identified can provide this evidence. A well-designed assessment plan should contain this information.

A common example of an invalid method would be a written test about a practical skill. This could produce knowledge and understanding evidence that is needed to underpin the practical skill – for example, changing a fuse – but it does not provide evidence that the candidate can actually perform the task. Unless this is complemented by observation of performance then the assessment, and, therefore, the evidence, is not valid.

### Reliability

Consistency of assessment within and between assessment centres is of central importance to the quality of an assessment system. The system will only be reliable if two assessors, presented with the same evidence, would make the same decision about the candidate's competence. A well-designed assessment system builds in checks of consistency and reliability and this is usually the responsibility of the internal verifier.

---

## ACTIVITY

How does your assessment centre meet the three conditions for effective assessment?

---

## FACTORS INFLUENCING ASSESSMENT DECISIONS

As an assessor you need to ensure that assessment is unobtrusive and does not interfere with normal workplace activity. This will ensure that any effect on performance by your presence will be kept to a minimum. There are other factors, however, that can affect the quality of an assessment system by influencing your judgement about a candidate's evidence. In order to maintain objectivity as an assessor you need to be aware of these potential influences. Below are some of the more common effects.

### Planned direction

Unplanned assessment can result in inaccurate judgements about the candidate's performance. If one or both of you are unclear about what is actually being assessed then the likelihood of a judgement of 'competent' is much reduced. Always be clear about what evidence is required from a particular assessment by referring to and being familiar with the specified performance standards.

## The illusion of validity

When observing someone or reviewing written evidence it is very easy to feel that 'this is good work'. The issue however is not whether or not the work is good but whether the evidence you are assessing provides valid proof that the required standards are being met. This means clearly identifying the standards of performance that you are assessing and comparing the evidence against those standards. If you become absorbed into the general work performance of the candidate then the evidence you are observing may be of high quality but irrelevant when judged against the performance criteria specified by the standards. This would produce invalid evidence and result in invalid assessment that would not fulfil the condition of reliability.

## Stereotyping

Stereotyping occurs when we make generalizations about a group of people. Assessment is about individual performance, and each candidate is assessed on their own merits. They may have a different ethnic background or religion, be male or female, disabled or able-bodied, full- or part-time, trainers or managers. This information has no relevance to any judgements you may make about their performance. Your concern is to collect and assess specific evidence of actual performance; in other words, to be objective.

## Hawthorn effect

The term 'Hawthorn effect' was coined as a result of some studies carried out in the 1950s by Elton Mayo. He discovered that a temporary improvement in performance can be observed when interest is shown in that performance. In the context of competence-based assessment this means that your observation of a candidate's performance could produce a beneficial effect on that performance. This should be countered, however, by the continuous nature of competence-based assessment. If assessment is carried out on a day-to-day basis, under normal working conditions, then this effect will be minimized.

## Halo and horns effect

Another source of inaccurate (or biased) judgement is as a result of our perception of the candidate as an individual. This may be because we like the person or know that they usually do good work (the halo effect). But it could equally be because we don't like the person or believe that their work is poor (the horns effect). These preconceived ideas about a candidate's performance can affect our judgement of that performance when we should be assessing it objectively, against specified standards.

## Contrast effects

Traditional assessment is often norm referenced (see chapter 1, p. 12) but competence-based assessment is individualized assessment. It is concerned with comparing the individual's performance to the specified standards, not with comparing the performance of one individual against that of another. When you are involved in assessing a number of candidates, therefore, you need to regard each one as an individual and avoid the temptation to make comparisons between their performances.

## Misleading information

This is more likely to be an issue if you are a second line assessor. In this role you are relying to a large extent on the judgements of other people. You need to be confident of their understanding of their role requirements and that they understand competence-based assessment and its requirements. An effective quality assurance model should minimize the occurrence of misleading or inaccurate information about a candidate's performance.

---

### ACTIVITY

Taking each of the factors in this section in turn, identify how you deal with them in your role as an assessor.

---

## ASSESSMENT METHODS

The assessment method or methods used will depend on a number of factors. They include:

- the type of evidence required;
- whether you are a first or second line assessor.

## Types of evidence

There are a bewildering number of terms used to describe the types of evidence you can collect and evaluate in a competence-based system. The more common forms of evidence are:

- performance
- knowledge
- primary
- secondary
- direct
- indirect
- historical
- supplementary
- supporting

Many of these terms are used interchangeably.

### Performance evidence

This refers specifically to evidence of an individual actually doing something. It is one form of direct evidence and is also one of the required primary forms of evidence. As a general rule performance evidence will be of a high quality.

### Knowledge evidence

This refers to evidence that indicates that the candidate can recall, transfer and apply knowledge within the working environment. This is also a primary form of evidence.

### Primary evidence

Primary types of evidence such as performance and knowledge evidence provide information about actual performance or the application of knowledge within normal workplace activity.

### Secondary, supporting or supplementary evidence

These terms refer to evidence that adds to the direct forms of evidence collected. They are usually indirect forms of evidence.

### Direct evidence

This refers to forms of evidence that give clear information about the candidate's actual performance. It includes the results of observation, questioning and the examination of products of performance. Products of performance simply means work produced as a result of performance. It is evidence produced *by* the candidate.

### Indirect evidence

This is evidence *about* the candidate and can take many forms. Assessors need to be particularly vigilant when evaluating indirect evidence and must remember to apply the rules of evidence identified earlier.

### Historical evidence

This is the principal method used for accreditation of prior learning (APL) (see below). It provides the assessor with information about the candidate's past achievements.

## First or second line assessor

As a first line assessor you will be mainly concerned with primary evidence. You will be concentrating on the collection and evaluation of performance and knowledge evidence relating to specific elements of competence. Secondary evidence will play a supplementary or supporting role in this process.

As a second line assessor, however, you will be required to evaluate a diverse range of evidence from secondary sources, as your role is more distant from the candidate. This could include evidence of prior learning or achievement. This is referred to as the accreditation of prior learning (APL) and relies on historical, secondary evidence.

## Primary and secondary evidence

For clarity evidence is usually classified as primary or secondary.
Primary sources include:

- performance in the workplace;
- work produced as a result of performance;
- results from questioning;
- simulation;
- videotape of the candidate's performance;
- audio tape of the candidate's performance.

Secondary sources include:

- results from questioning others about the candidate's performance, sometimes referred to as witness testimony;
- results of skill tests;
- project reports;
- assignments;
- written reports;
- work reports;
- photographs of work produced;
- letters of validation;
- references and testimonials;
- results of self-assessments;
- training and development records;
- appraisal reports;
- awards and certificates.

## Choosing appropriate methods

As an assessor, there are a number of methods of evidence collection and evaluation available to you.

### Observation of performance at work

This should always be the primary method of evidence collection. Competence-based assessment aims to measure performance outcomes and the best source of high quality evidence therefore is the workplace. We said earlier in the chapter that your presence in the normal working environment should be unobtrusive. This is to ensure that your presence has as little influence on the performance of the candidate as is possible.

### Questioning

It is unlikely that observation on its own will provide sufficient evidence to infer competence. You have to ensure that the candidate also has the relevant knowledge and understanding that underpins the demonstration of skill. Asking 'why?' questions, for example, 'Why did you use brainstorming for that activity?' will allow the candidate to provide evidence that they understand and can use relevant knowledge. Questions can be presented orally or in written form. If a written format is used the assessor should be present while they are completed.

### Skills and/or knowledge tests

These are a source of limited evidence as they focus on a one-off demonstration of skills or knowledge. They can be useful as supplementary evidence.

### Projects, assignments and simulations

Occasionally, candidates may be unable to provide performance evidence in the workplace across the full range required by the specified standards. This could be because the full range of activity does not occur in that particular workplace. It could also be that every effort is made to prevent a particular activity occurring, for example, a fire. Any simulation should closely resemble normal workplace conditions for it to have validity.

### Product examination

This is another essential part of assessment. It requires the examination of the products or outputs generated by workplace performance.

### Discussions with third parties

This could include discussions with a candidate's manager or peers about the candidate's performance. It will usually provide secondary evidence, although if the activity being assessed is a sensitive one where the presence of an assessor might be a problem – providing counselling, for example – then a discussion with the person counselled could provide primary evidence. This obviously needs to be handled with care, however.

### Document examination

The examination of documents such as witness testimonies, certificates, letters of validation, etc, can provide useful supplementary evidence to support a claim of competence.

---

## ACTIVITY

Compile a list of questions that you could ask yourself when choosing assessment methods.

---

For the Activity exercise your list could have included the following:

- What evidence is required?
- How much evidence is required?

- Can it be gained from normal workplace activity?
- How much time is there available?
- Which methods could provide suitable evidence?
- Are they cost-effective?
- Are they practical?
- Do the methods meet the rules of assessment methods?
- Will the evidence meet the rules of evidence?
- Which methods are least disruptive?
- Can I competently use the methods?
- Can I become competent?
- Can someone else do the assessment?

## SECOND LINE ASSESSMENT

The second line assessor is concerned with assessing competence using more diverse forms of evidence than the first line assessor. You may also be working with a number of first line assessors and you may be providing advice and support to both candidates and workplace assessors. Second line assessors are responsible for 'signing off' units of competence, usually presented in portfolio format.

### The portfolio

As you will be assessing the portfolio you will probably want to offer help and guidance to the candidate in the preparation of it. An NVQ or SVQ portfolio is produced by the candidate and consists mainly of documents. These documents may have been produced by the candidate or will contain information about the candidate. Other products may also be included such as video tapes, photographs and certificates. It may also include evidence of prior achievement.

The portfolio will need to be well indexed, cross-referenced and have contents that are clear, logical, comprehensive and relevant. As part of the quality assurance process the internal verifier will sample portfolios. It is important therefore that the portfolio can be easily followed by someone not involved with its preparation. All of these conditions are the responsibility of the candidate, not the assessor, and this needs to be made clear to the candidate at the outset.

The role of the second line assessor is quite a complex one, therefore, and requires mastery of a wide range of assessment methods.

## RECORDING DECISIONS

At first glance this may seem a straightforward activity. You make a decision based on the evidence you have reviewed as to whether the candidate is competent, not yet competent or there is insufficient evidence to make a judgement. Once you have made this decision you then record it in whatever way the awarding body or organization requires. Competence-based assessment is a continuous process, however, and, as such, developmental. This can result in a number of decisions being made as an outcome of an assessment and they will need to be recorded. The four most common types of information that should be recorded are:

- evidence;
- achievement;
- training needs identified;
- training provision identified.

## Recording evidence

Awarding bodies often have their own documentation for the recording of evidence. If yours does not, or you are using standards devised by the organization then you will need to develop your own system. Any system for recording evidence needs to be both simple to use and efficient as it needs to be accessible to the candidate as well as the assessor. You need to be able to record for each element:

- what evidence has been collected;
- where the evidence was collected;
- when it was collected;
- the method of assessment used;
- who carried out the assessment;
- when the competence in the element is achieved;
- confirmation that the candidate has received feedback on the assessment.

As this record may be used as the basis for recommendation of an award it is essential that it is compatible with and supports the quality assurance system. It needs, therefore, to be a comprehensive record that is easily accessible and can be sampled by the second line assessor or internal verifier.

## Recording achievement

Whereas recording evidence is concerned with assessment decisions at element level, recording achievement records decisions at unit level. Awarding bodies will only record a candidate's achievement at unit level. Once all the elements for a particular unit have been judged competent the second line assessor then has to make a judgement as to whether the amalgamated evidence meets all the requirements of the unit, particularly with regard to the range. A judgement of 'competent' then results in an award of the specified unit. If the candidate is not working towards the whole NVQ or SVQ, then a record of achievement is usually issued detailing which units have been achieved.

The procedure for recording achievement and initiating the formal record of achievement is usually laid down by the awarding body. If you are using standards developed by an organization you will need to ensure that a suitable system for recording achievement is in place.

## Recording identified training needs

As the process of assessment gets under way it is likely that the assessor, with the candidate, will identify some gaps in performance evidence. This may be for one of two reasons: either through a lack of opportunity to demonstrate competence because of restrictions imposed by work role; or through lack of the skills, knowledge and/or understanding required to perform to the specified standard. As a result of this, training needs will be identified and it is important that those needs are formally recorded.

Failure to record training needs identified during the assessment process may result in a number of consequences, including an inability to gain the award and a loss of motivation by the candidate. By formally recording the training need you can then pass the information on to the appropriate person in the organization so that appropriate action can be taken to fill the gap.

## Recording identified training provision

In order to complement the competence-based assessment approach the organization will also need to cater for competence-based development needs. As an assessor you will need to be familiar with the training and development provision available within the organization. This will include information on modular programmes based on clearly specified standards of performance as well as the opportunities available for coaching and other on-the-job methods. (See chapter 5 p. 80.)

By recording the action to be taken to fill any gaps in the candidate's competence all relevant parties will be aware of what is required. This should result in an almost seamless process of development and assessment for the candidate. It should also result in the award being obtained in the optimum amount of time by avoiding unnecessary delays in the process.

## Feedback

It is important to stress yet again that the feedback resulting from the decision-making process must be given to the candidate in an appropriate and timely manner. The recording system is simply a procedure for ensuring that adequate records are kept for reference and certification purposes. The emphasis of the assessment process is on the candidate's performance and it is vital that decisions arising from that process are fed back with care and sensitivity.

---

### ACTIVITY

Identify the assessment recording systems used within your assessment centre or organization and compare them against the criteria identified here. If you feel they could be improved discuss this with the internal verifier.

---

## SUMMARY

Competence-based development and assessment requires assessors to be competent themselves in a number of specific areas. This chapter has highlighted the areas relevant to first and second line assessors operating within a competence-based system.

It began by identifying the assessment and verification roles to be found within a competence-based system. The competence-based quality assurance system was identified and you were encouraged to identify how the system works in your organization or assessment centre. The assessment process was then described along with a number of key decisions to be made by assessors. The requirements of the assessment plan were also identified here.

Following on from this was the collection and assessment of evidence. The rules of evidence were identified along with the rules of assessment methods and their application in the workplace. The focus here was on the objective nature of competence-based assessment and, conse-quently, the factors influencing assessment decisions were also discussed.

Types and sources of evidence were discussed next and clarification given about the multitude of terms used to describe competence-based evidence. These types were condensed into two categories, primary and secondary evidence, and methods available to the assessor to collect appropriate evidence were then highlighted. Factors that need to be considered by assessors when choosing assessment methods were also discussed here.

The specific requirements of second line assessment followed, with particular attention being paid to the use of portfolios for assessment.

The competence-based assessment process can result in a number of decisions being made about the candidate's current competence and current and future development needs. The importance of recording these decisions in an appropriate format was highlighted here, along with the implications for candidate feedback.

### Further useful reading

Fletcher, S (1992) *Competence-based Assessment Techniques*, Kogan Page, London.

Marshall, J (1993) *Portfolio Development Towards National Standards: A Guide for Candidates, Advisers and Assessors*, Development Processes, Manchester.

Ollin, R and Tucker, J (1994) *The NVQ and GNVQ Assessor Handbook*, Kogan Page, London.

Parsloe, E (1992) *Coaching, Mentoring and Assessing. A Practical Guide to Developing Competence*, Kogan Page, London.

Redman, W (1994) *Portfolios for Development. A Guide for Trainers and Managers*, Kogan Page, London.

Simosko, S (1991) *APL: A Practical Guide for Professionals*, Kogan Page, London.

Walklin, L (1991) *The Assessment of Performance and Competence: A Handbook for Teachers and Trainers*, Stanley Thornes, London.

# Bibliography

Allender, S (1991) *Report Writing*, BACIE, London.

Anderson, A H (1993) *Successful Training Practice: A Manager's Guide to Personnel Development*, Blackwell, Oxford.

Applegarth, M (1991) *How to Take a Training Audit*, Kogan Page, London.

Becker, P (1993) *Powerful Presentation Skills*, Addison Wesley, Massachusetts.

Bell, A H (1990) *Mastering the Meeting Maze*, Addison Wesley, Massachusetts.

Boydell, T H (1992) *Guide to the Identification of Training Needs*, BACIE, London.

Bramley, P (1990) *Evaluating Training Effectiveness: Translating Theory into Practice*, McGraw Hill, London.

Bramley, P (1990) *Evaluation of Training: A Practical Guide*, BACIE, London.

Broad, M L and Newstrom, J W (1992) *Transfer of Training: Action Packed Strategies to Ensure High Payoff from Training Investments*, Addison Wesley, Massachusetts.

Buckley, R and Caple, J (1991) *One-to-one Training and Coaching Skills*, Kogan Page, London.

Buckley, R and Caple, J (1994) *The Theory and Practice of Training*, third edition, Kogan Page, London.

Calder, J (1994) *Programme Evaluation and Quality: A Comprehensive Guide to Setting up an Evaluation System*, Kogan Page, London.

Clark, N (1992) *Managing Personal Learning and Change: A Trainer's Guide*, McGraw Hill, London.

Clements, P and Spinks, T (1993) *A Practical Guide to Facilitation Skills*, Kogan Page, London.

Cockman, P Evans, B and Reynolds, P (1994) *Client-centred Consulting: A Practical Guide for Internal Advisors and Trainers*, McGraw Hill, London.

Coopers and Lybrand Associates (1985) *A Challenge to Complacency*, MSC/NEDO, Sheffield.

Cotton, J (1995) *The Theory of Learning*, Kogan Page, London.

Cushway, B and Lodge, D (1993) *Organizational Behaviour and Design*, Kogan Page, London.

Davis, J (1992) *How to Write a Training Manual*, Gower, Aldershot.

Easterby Smith, M (1994) *Evaluating Management Development, Training and Development*, Gower, Aldershot.

Ehrenborg, J and Mattock, J (1993) *Powerful Presentations. 50 Original Ideas for Making a Real Impact*, Kogan Page, London.

Employment Department (1992) *National Training Awards Prospectus*, HMSO, London.

Flegg, D and McHale, J (1991) *Selecting Training Aids*, Kogan Page, London.

Fletcher, J (1995) *Conducting Effective Interviews*, Kogan Page, London.

Fletcher, S (1991) *Designing Competence-based Training*, Kogan Page, London.

Fletcher, S (1992) *Competence-based Assessment Techniques*, Kogan Page, London.

Fletcher, S (1993) *Quality and Competence*, Kogan Page, London.

Fletcher, S (1994) *NVQs, Standards and Competence*, second edition, Kogan Page, London.

Gill, J and Johnson, P (1991) *Research Methods for Managers*, Paul Chapman Publishing, London.

Hamblin, A C (1974) *Evaluation and Control of Training*, McGraw Hill, London.

Handy, C B (1993) *Understanding Organizations*, third edition, Penguin, London.

Harrison, R (1992) *Employee Development*, IPM, London.

Hart, L B (1992) *Training Methods that Work*, Kogan Page, London.

Haynes, M E (1988) *Effective Meeting Skills*, Kogan Page, London.

Honey, P and Mumford, A (1986) *Using Your Learning Styles*, second edition, Honey, Maidenhead.

Honey, P and Mumford, A (1992) *Manual of Learning Styles*, third edition, Honey, Maidenhead.

Huczynski, A and Buchanan, D (1991) *Organizational Behaviour*, second edition, Prentice Hall, London.

Jackson, T (1989) *Evaluation. Relating Training to Performance*, Kogan Page, London.

Kirkpatrick, D L (1976) 'Evaluation of Training' in Craig, R L (ed.) *Training and Development Handbook*, McGraw Hill, London.

Kolb, D A, Rubin, I M and McIntyre, J M (1974) *Organizational Psychology: An Experiential Approach*, Prentice Hall, New Jersey.

Leigh, D (1991) *A Practical Approach to Group Training*, Kogan Page, London.

Maddux, R B (1988) *Successful Negotiation*, Kogan Page, London.

Mager, R (1991) *Developing Attitudes Towards Learning*, second edition, Kogan Page, London.

Mager, R (1991) *Making Instruction Work*, Kogan Page, London.

Mager, R (1991) *Measuring Instructional Results*, second edition, Kogan Page, London.

Mager, R and Pipe, P (1991) *Analysing Performance Problems*, second edition, Kogan Page, London.

Manchester Open Learning (1993) *Handling Conflict and Negotiation*, Kogan Page, London.

Manchester Open Learning (1993) *Making Effective Presentations*, Kogan Page, London.

Mandel, S (1993) *Effective Presentation Skills*, revised edition, Kogan Page, London.

Manpower Services Commission (1981) *Glossary of Training Terms*, MSC, HMSO, London.

Marshall, J (1993) *Portfolio Development towards National Standards: A Guide for Candidates, Advisers and Assessors*, Development Processes, Manchester.

MCI (1991) *Occupational Standards for Managers*, MCI, London.

Moss, G (1993) *The Trainer's Desk Reference*, second edition, Kogan Page, London.

NCVQ (1988) *Information Note 4 (November)* NCVQ, London.

Newby, T (1992) *Cost Effective Training*, Kogan Page, London.

Newby, T (1992) *Validating your Training*, Kogan Page, London.

Nicolay, C and Barrette, J (1992) *Assembling Course Materials*, Kogan Page, London.

NVQ Communications (1993) *Skillscan: Training and Development, Level 4*, HMSO, London.

Ollin, R and Tucker, J (1994) *The NVQ and GNVQ Assessor Handbook*, Kogan Page, London.

Owen, M (1991) *Productive Presentations*, BACIE, London.

Parsloe, E (1992) *Coaching, Mentoring and Assessing. A Practical Guide to Developing Competence*, Kogan Page, London.

Peel, M (1988) *How to Make Meetings Work*, Kogan Page, London.

Pepper, A D (1987) *Managing the Training and Development Function*, Gower, Aldershot.

Peterson, R (1992) *Training Needs Analysis in the Workplace*, Kogan Page, London.

Philips, J (1991) *Handbook of Training Evaluation and Measurement Methods*, second edition, Kogan Page, London.

Phillips, K and Shaw, P (1989) *A Consultancy Approach for Trainers*, Gower, Aldershot.

Pont, T (1990) *Developing Effective Training Skills*, McGraw Hill, London.

Powers, B (1992) *Instructor Excellence*, Jossey-Bass Publishers, San Francisco.

Prior, J (ed.) (1991) *Gower Handbook of Training and Development*, Gower, Aldershot.

Rae, L (1991) *How to Measure Training Effectiveness*, second edition, Gower, Aldershot.

Rae, L (1993) *The Skills of Training. A Guide for Managers and Practitioners*, second edition, Gower, Adlershot.

Redman, W (1994) *Portfolios for Development. A Guide for Trainers and Managers*, Kogan Page, London.

Reeves, M (1993) *Evaluation of Training*, The Industrial Society, London.

Reid, M, Barrington, H and Kenney, J (1992) *Training Interventions*, third edition, IPM, London.

Robinson, C (1995) *Effective Negotiation*, Kogan Page, London.

Robinson, K (1989) *A Handbook of Training Management*, second edition, Kogan Page, London.

Russel, T (1994) *Effective Feedback Skills*, Kogan Page, London.

Saunders, M and Holdaway, K (1992) *The In-house Trainer as Consultant*, Kogan Page, London.

Sheal, P (1994) *How to Develop and Present Staff Training Courses*, second edition, Kogan Page, London.

Simosko, S (1991) *APL: A Practical Guide for Professionals*, Kogan Page, London.

Stevens, M (1987) *Improving your Presentation Skills. A Complete Action Kit*, Kogan Page, London.

Stimson, N (1991) *How to Write and Prepare Training Materials*, Kogan Page, London.

Stout, S (1992) *Managing Training*, Kogan Page, London.

Truelove, S (ed.) (1992) *Handbook of Training and Development*, Blackwell, Oxford.

Vicar, R (1994) *How to Speak and Write Persuasively*, Kogan Page, London.

Walklin, L (1991) *The Assessment of Performance and Competence: A Handbook for Teachers and Trainers*, Stanley Thornes, London.

Walmsley, H (1994) *Counselling Techniques for Managers*, Kogan Page, London.

Warr, P, Bird, M and Rackham, N (1979) *Evaluation of Management Training*, sixth edition, Gower, Aldershot.

# Index